a salad
for all seasons

Harry Eastwood first came to the public's attention in 2007 when she co-presented Channel 4's popular prime-time television series *Cook Yourself Thin*. She later went on to present the twenty-part US version of the show on Lifetime network. Since then, she has published two books, *Red Velvet & Chocolate Heartache* and *The Skinny French Kitchen*.

Harry recently moved back to Paris after spending a year in London writing *A Salad for All Seasons*. She is currently working on various features and a new book. She is also a frequent presenter of the cookery segment on the daily TV show *C'est Au Programme* in France.

She loves chocolate more than ever.

a salad
for all seasons

harry eastwood

BANTAM PRESS

LONDON · TORONTO · SYDNEY · AUCKLAND · JOHANNESBURG

for the filles,
femmes and friends
who fill my life
with fun.

th x

TRANSWORLD PUBLISHERS
61–63 Uxbridge Road, London W5 5SA
A Random House Group Company
www.transworldbooks.co.uk

First published in Great Britain
in 2013 by Bantam Press
an imprint of Transworld Publishers

A CIP catalogue record for this book
is available from the British Library.

ISBN 9780593069943

Addresses for Random House Group Ltd companies outside the UK
can be found at: www.randomhouse.co.uk
The Random House Group Ltd Reg. No. 954009

The Random House Group Limited supports the Forest Stewardship Council® (FSC®), the
leading international forest-certification organisation. Our books carrying the FSC label are
printed on FSC®-certified paper. FSC is the only forest-certification scheme supported by
the leading environmental organisations, including Greenpeace. Our paper procurement
policy can be found at www.randomhouse.co.uk/environment.

Photography: **Laura Edwards**
Design: **Lucy Gowans**
Art direction: **Tabitha Hawkins** and **Harry Eastwood**
Food styling: **Joss Herd** and **Danny Maguire**
Props styling: **Tabitha Hawkins**
Nutritional information: **Judith Wills**

Typeset in Big Caslon and Adobe Caslon Pro and Helvetica Neue
Printed and bound in Great Britain by **Butler, Tanner & Dennis Ltd**, Frome

2 4 6 8 10 9 7 5 3 1

Contents

Spring is bursting with delicate flowers,

fresh asparagus, butter-coloured new potatoes

and the defiance of young leaves; Summer

is exuberant and full of light, bright, playful colours;

dim the lights for Autumn, which marks the

beginning of mushroom, chestnut, wild game and

pumpkin season; dark   greens and

purples are spiked with pomegranate pink

to keep up the spirit, and warm salads

soothe from the cold.

A Salad by Any Other Name . . .

When I was a little girl growing up in France, I hankered after two
British staples: white plastic bread and iceberg lettuce. My grandparents
used to take my sister Georgie and me to the cinema in Bognor Regis as
a treat. We lunched in a caff where they served cheese sandwiches with
a side salad, followed by a cup of tea and a chocolate digestive – all for
under £10 between the four of us. I remember the 'salad' because it was
so different to French salads, being made up of iceberg lettuce and soggy
tomatoes with salad cream artfully draped over the top. In England
twenty years ago that's pretty much what salads looked like wherever you
went . . . how things have changed!

To me, a 'salad' is now characterized by a couple of key words:
imagination, simplicity and fresh, seasonal ingredients. I eat a different
salad every single day. Some days I'm using warmed-up leftovers and
some days I'm crunching down on mostly leaves. Some days it's a side
salad and some days it's the main event. I regularly make salads for
dinner parties, as well as for TV suppers on my own. The joy of a salad is
that it can be made up from almost anything and it will always provide
you with a healthy, colourful and fun food experience.

A Salad for All Seasons is a book you will eat with your eyes,
a book of recipes that will get your heart beating faster –
because not only are the recipes exciting and beautiful,
they are also quick and *do-able*.

My aim in this book has been to share
my love of salad and of eating delicious
food that also makes you *feel good*.

I like the fact that most of the salads in this book will effortlessly give you two or more of your five-a-day – the fun way! To make things easier, you will find the magic number at the top of each recipe. The really virtuous salads (the ones that are lowest in calories and highest in vegetables) can be identified by a little halo symbol. There are twenty-one of these dotted throughout the book.

A salad a day = variet-ay

With this in mind, this book is full of ideas and recipes to inspire *you* to make salads a regular part of your life too. Apart from being delicious, salads are also a way of looking at leaves and vegetables in a fresh, new light. At the end of this introduction, I have included a small selection of my favourite seasonal leaves to look out for and a brief note on how to best use them in your recipes. Some of these leaves and shoots will already be familiar to you, but hopefully some won't. The recipes in this book are as much about new ways of looking at familiar ingredients as they are ideas and techniques I have been gathering together from all over the world of food.

My only rule when cooking is to make food that excites, delights and nourishes me. In *A Salad for All Seasons* you can expect to find recipes that are simple, delicious and ready in five minutes, like **Grilled Avocado and Cherry Tomato with Lime and Coriander**, as well as recipes like **Southern Salad with Root Beer Brisket** that benefit from being made the day before. You will find salads inspired from my travels abroad, like **Thai Beef and Basil with Glass Noodles**, and some that remind me of home, like **English Garden Salad of Peas, Shoots, Smoked Trout and Horseradish**. There are classic salad combinations such as **Roast Chicken Caesar Salad** as well as outlandish ones like **A Salad of Mushrooms and Deep-fried Egg**. I have included a **Store-cupboard Salad** for each season, as well as a handful of

fruit salads. All the recipes in this book rely on seasonal ingredients because, when it comes to salads, it's all about fresh, lively ingredients in their prime.

Vegetarian variations

A lot of the recipes naturally sprang up vegetarian – more by accident than by design. I found that at least half the recipes I dreamt up just happened not to include meat. They didn't seem to need any extra gilding once the right vegetables, textures and dressing had come together. Even in salads that include meat, you will often find a vegetarian variation at the end of the recipe. This is partly because salads are inherently versatile and partly because eating meat is a personal choice. I respect that a large number of people are cutting back on their meat consumption for ecological, ethical and health reasons.

The importance of dressing right

Salad leaves and dressings require the same careful pairings as the Italians give to pasta shapes and sauce. Indeed, dressing clings to leaves in much the same way and an overdressed, soggy salad is a drab, sad sight.

'Dressing' is exactly the right word in the context of a salad, because a different vinaigrette can completely alter the look, taste and texture of a plate of leaves. The brilliant news here is that you can tip a bag of mixed leaves into a bowl and add four different dressings on four different days and experience an entirely different meal each time. In addition to the dressings I have paired with each individual recipe, I have included a set of four different stock vinaigrettes to use on your own salad recipes (pages 188–9).

There are many wonderful vinegars and glazes already available in most supermarkets and delis, but they tend to be rather expensive. For the gourmets amongst you, or for those who, like me, enjoy giving presents I've made myself, there is also a section with recipes for home-made infused vinegars – **Raspberry, Honey and Tarragon, Thyme and Tangerine** or **Cucumber and Pink Peppercorn** – which will spruce up even the simplest salad on pages 192–3.

Glazes are a fantastic way of jazzing up a last-minute salad or a warm plate of vegetables and you will find three different recipes for home-made glazes on pages 186–7.

Pestos are often overlooked as a great way of dressing salads, especially vegetarian salads or those that include fish. On pages 190–1 you will also find recipes for **Hazelnut Pesto, Red Pepper Pesto** and **Lime and Coriander Pesto**. Once made, I use them as dips and as sauces for pasta, as well as a fabulous way of pepping up a simple salad.

The times they are a-changin' . . .

The seasons have changed so much in the last few years that it's difficult to pin down where summer stops and autumn begins, or when autumn turns into winter. I've devised the recipe selection in this book to include recipes that *I feel like eating* at that time of year (a kind of emotional seasonality), as well, of course, as looking at what's available in the local markets around where I have been living in Richmond. I couldn't resist including the recipe for **Pan-fried Bananas with Rum Butterscotch** in the Autumn chapter, despite the fact that bananas simply aren't farmed in the UK (although I did read somewhere recently that a fella in Maidenhead has successfully managed to grow a group of banana trees in his back garden, by protecting them from the winter cold!).

The importance of eating seasonal produce is simply that it is at its best, and therefore tastes better and has more nutrients. The trouble for a city-dweller like me who doesn't have a garden in which to grow my own fruit and vegetables is that supermarkets are such pros when it comes to making ingredients available all year round that you have to be a very vigilant customer if you want to avoid adding haricot beans from Kenya and apples from New Zealand to your trolley. I found the websites www.nationaltrust.org. uk/what-we-do/food-and-farming and www.eattheseasons. co.uk to be fantastic rough guides to what's in season when I was unsure of exactly when British raspberries ceased to be harvested.

Bringing back fast food

When I set out to write this book, I thought of a salad as being a dish made up mainly of vegetables, whether hot or cold, and invariably including some sort of leaves. I have discovered that although this holds true, the soul of a great salad lies in the freshness of its ingredients, the imagination with which it comes together and the vibrancy of the colours, textures and tastes on your plate.

To my delight, I have found that eating a salad a day has opened up a world of lunches and dinners that are decadent and satisfying – and usually knocked up in twenty minutes. So to make things easier you will find a clock symbol at the top of all recipes that are super quick to make. *A Salad for All Seasons* is proof that food that is natural, quick and healthy can also be a feast. This is a book about exceptional, vibrant, stylish . . . fast food.

Finalement

I debated whether or not to include calorie counts in this book and finally decided to add them to the top of each recipe because so many people find them useful. However, I'm less interested in calories than I used to be; what matters more to me is that this book will introduce you to naturally healthy ingredients in a fresh, new light. Enjoying salads is the best way I know to make hitting those 'five-a-day' easy, colourful and fun – every time.

Dictionary of Leaves
Spring

*Baby lettuce leaves such as baby green or red romaine and baby green or red oak leaf are **tender** and **feather-light**. Even the darker leaves that tend to have more bite are still very **mild** when so young.*

Baby lettuce leaves also marry well with more crispy salad ingredients like croutons, bacon, toasted nuts or crunchy leaves such as cos.

These versatile little leaves are perfect with sharp ingredients like radish or mustard- and vinegar-based dressings.

Summer

WATERCRESS *is **peppery** and slightly **bitter**. Delicious mixed with fruit or cream-based dressings. Watercress likes to be surrounded by crunchy textures, as its leaves are **fragile** and wilt easily.*

BABY RUBY CHARD *has a slightly earthy flavour but is a **peppy**, **light** little leaf that tastes similar to baby spinach. Ruby chard is a personal favourite because it's very pretty and is a great all-rounder.*

DANDELION *is **spiky** and super **bitter**. Use in small amounts alongside herbs, chilli and other big flavours. Its hardy stem means that it mixes well with soft ingredients like flowers, Mozzarella or ricotta. Delicious in warm salads, slightly **wilted**.*

LITTLE GEM *is used for its wonderful **crunchiness** and as a vehicle for other stronger flavours, as well as for 'catching' dressing.*

EDIBLE FLOWERS *are a treat, in season only for a short period. Nothing but nothing makes a salad look more **beautiful** than a few flowers dotted over the top. Popular edible varieties in the UK include nasturtiums (slightly **peppery**) or violas (slightly **sweet**).*

I love **TOPS**, whether **BEET**
or **SPROUT** or **CELERY**.

They come 'free' with the bulbs and
are wonderful chopped up as a salad
leaf. As expected, these beetroot tops
have a strong **earthy** taste and **hardy**,
rich, **green** leaves. Taste as though
they're doing you good (which, of
course, they are!).

PAK CHOI *is super-**crispy**, with soft green leaves that taste very faintly of **cabbage**. Great with **Asian** flavours, as well as used **wilted** in warm salads.*

CHICORY *(also called 'endive') is often used in French recipes and grows more **bitter** the closer you get to the heart. The red variety is slightly sweeter than the white. Chicory is delicious with goat's or blue cheese, softened fruit like pears or sweet vegetables like pumpkin, in both hot and cold salads.*

Winter

OAK LEAF LETTUCE *is a wonderful vehicle for dressings with its* **mild** *tasting, open,* **frilly leaves.** *The* **soft** *oak leaves are perfect for crunchy ingredients like toasted nuts, croutons and crispy bacon, as well as rich flavours like liver and game.*

RADICCHIO *is often used in Italian cooking and can be served* **cooked** *or raw alongside hot ingredients. It is very well suited to winter fruit like figs and pears, as well as soft cheeses and rich meats, because its* **sharpness** *helps to restore the flavour balance.*

SPINACH *is the most **useful** of all leaves. A handful of spinach gives you a **subtle-flavoured** green hit of goodness and freshness. Tastes great with everything.*

Spring

This recipe has already become a family favourite with my aunt and cousin next door because it's so quick to rustle up and so scrumptious. They prefer it with more gnocchetti and less asparagus, whilst I tend to load up my plate with green stems and dot the gnocchi over as a bit of an afterthought. As ever, it's entirely up to you how you choose to eat yours.

335 cals per portion
2 of your five-a-day per portion

Asparagus, Gnocchetti and Prosciutto with lemon and crème fraîche dressing

Serves 2

340g asparagus tips (i.e. without the woody ends)

150g gnocchetti (baby gnocchi), or regular size if you can't find the smaller varieties

2 tsp olive oil

100g prosciutto

zest of ½ unwaxed lemon

3 tbsp half-fat crème fraîche

a few sprigs roughly chopped parsley

plenty of salt and black pepper

Drop the asparagus tips in boiling water and bring back to the boil. Remove them from the saucepan with a slotted spoon. If the asparagus are thick, cut them in half lengthways before setting aside. You're literally just blanching them briefly, as they get cooked again in the pan later.

Cook the gnocchetti in the asparagus water, according to packet instructions. Once drained, drizzle over 1 tsp of olive oil and set aside.

Fry the prosciutto in a dry frying pan (non-stick is easiest) until golden and crispy. Remove and set aside to cool.

Fire up the frying pan until hot and add the asparagus, the remaining 1 tsp of olive oil and the lemon zest. Fry over a high heat for 2–3 minutes or until they begin to warm through and colour.

Divide the asparagus and gnocchetti between two plates, then add the crème fraîche over the top. Crumble over the prosciutto, followed by a sprinkling of parsley and a crunch of pepper. Scatter any residual lemon zest over for a final hit of yellow.

Swap in ... Bow-tie pasta instead of gnocchetti, pancetta instead of prosciutto, sage instead of parsley (in which case add it to the pan with the asparagus at the end). You can add shaved Parmesan or Pecorino and nutmeg instead of the ham if you don't want to use meat in this recipe.

I'm not much of a forager but there is something amazing about food you picked yourself – not to mention the fact that it's *free*. The good news is that dandelions grow everywhere and the leaves are really distinctive, so you know you won't get it wrong. They're very bitter-tasting, a bit like certain types of rocket, so it's worth mixing them with sweeter varieties of leaves. I aim for one dandelion leaf in ten others because of the strength of the flavour. And I use the yellow petals because they're so pretty.

410 calories per portion
2 of your five-a-day

Avocado, Dandelion and Devilled Seeds

Serves 2

a dozen small dandelion leaves

4 yellow dandelion flowers

½ tsp vegetable oil

¼ tsp Worcestershire sauce

1½ tsp soft brown sugar

¼ tsp salt

a pinch cayenne pepper

60g mixed seeds

2 large handfuls mixed baby lettuce leaves, washed and dried

1 small avocado, cut into thin strips

For the dressing

1 tbsp olive oil

2 tsp freshly squeezed lemon juice

2 tsp red wine vinegar

a little salt for seasoning

Wash the dandelion leaves thoroughly, then lay them out on a tea towel to dry.

To make the devilled seeds, mix the oil, Worcestershire sauce, sugar, salt and cayenne pepper in a small saucepan over a medium flame. Add the seeds and toast until golden. Set aside to cool whilst you make the dressing.

Mix the dressing ingredients together in a clean jam jar and give a good shake.

Finally, toss the salad leaves, avocado and dandelion leaves lightly in the dressing and scatter the seeds over.

Finish by tearing the petals from the dandelion flowers and sprinkling them over the top. Serve immediately.

Swap in ... If you're not a fan of the dandelion, this salad is also great with a mixture of rocket and lettuce. I like it with a ball of Mozzarella on the side to offer a milky, tender contrast to all that spike.

Spring vegetables are much sweeter and more tender than later ones because they're only little and have just come out of the ground. As a rule, the best way to handle them is: don't over-complicate things. Stellette is a subtle and unobtrusive type of pasta that doesn't bog down the vegetables with starch or weight. I've chosen a light dressing, but you could just as easily toss the salad in a little butter and some freshly chopped mint.

385 calories per portion
2 of your five-a-day

Baby Spring Vegetables, Stellette and Parmesan

Serves 2

80g stellette pasta (they look like tiny little stars)

2 tbsp olive oil

120g baby sugar snap peas, sliced on the diagonal

120g baby carrots, topped, tailed and shaved with a potato-peeler

120g baby courgettes, topped, tailed and shaved with a potato-peeler

a handful tarragon, finely chopped

2 tsp freshly squeezed lemon juice

plenty of salt and black pepper

30g Parmesan, grated

2 tsp Balsamic Glaze (shop-bought, or see page 186)

Boil the stellette in a large frying pan (don't worry – I did mean a frying pan, not a saucepan) until *just* cooked.

Drain the water from the pasta and add the olive oil along with the prepared vegetables. Cover the pan with a lid for 2 minutes to heat the vegetables through. They will be barely cooked.

Add the tarragon and lemon juice and toss to combine. Season generously with salt and black pepper. Sprinkle with the Parmesan and drizzle over a trickle of the Balsamic Glaze. Serve straight away.

Swap in ... Boiled new potatoes or chicken instead of the pasta. If you can't find stellette you could swap in orzo. Add lemon zest and fried sage to the recipe and take out the tarragon. I also suggest substituting mint and chives for the tarragon. You could swap the sugar snaps for garden peas and the Parmesan for Pecorino.

My years in France have instilled in me a love of the sour salad leaves like endive and frisée. The whiter the leaves, the less sun they have had and the more bitter they tend to be. Some of the outside leaves of a frisée are greenish, but mostly it's a spiky, pale-looking salad leaf. Nothing marries as well with this particular type of sourness, in my view, as bacon, or the soothing comfort of a soft-boiled egg.

470 calories per portion
1 of your five-a-day

Breakfast Salad of bacon, eggs, fried bread and frisée

Serves 2

120g lardons

100g stale bread, broken into chunks

a little salt and black pepper

2 large free-range eggs

a small head frisée lettuce, escarole or any other bitter leaf, washed and dried

1 small banana shallot, cut into tiny dice

For the dressing

1 tsp Dijon mustard

1 tsp mayonnaise (I like Hellmann's)

1 tsp olive oil

1 tbsp half-fat crème fraîche

1 tsp white wine vinegar

Set a full kettle on to boil.

Heat the lardons in a large frying pan over a medium-high heat until golden and crispy. Remove with a slotted spoon and set aside.

Add the stale bread to the pan with the lardon juices and season with a little salt and pepper. Once the bread is crunchy and coloured, turn off the heat and set aside. Do not wash the pan.

Meanwhile, lower the eggs into boiling water and cook for exactly 6 minutes. This will ensure you have a cooked egg with a runny middle.

Next, whisk the mustard, mayonnaise, olive oil and crème fraîche in the now empty frying pan until combined. Thin down the dressing with the vinegar then taste and season.

Toss the salad leaves into the pan and coat them with the dressing before dividing between two plates. Scatter the lardons, fried bread and diced shallot over the top.

Peel the eggs and cut in half. Set on top of the finished salad with a crunch of black pepper. Serve warm.

Swap in ... Replace the lardon pan juices with 1 tsp vegetable oil and use sunblush tomatoes straight from the jar instead of lardons for a vegetarian option.

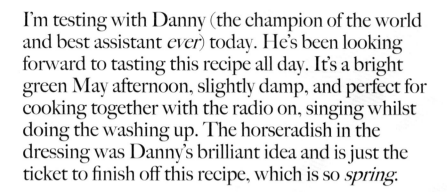

I'm testing with Danny (the champion of the world and best assistant *ever*) today. He's been looking forward to tasting this recipe all day. It's a bright green May afternoon, slightly damp, and perfect for cooking together with the radio on, singing whilst doing the washing up. The horseradish in the dressing was Danny's brilliant idea and is just the ticket to finish off this recipe, which is so *spring*.

277 calories per portion
1 of your five-a-day

English Garden Salad
of peas, shoots, smoked trout and horseradish

Serves 4

300g baby new potatoes

250g garden peas (fresh or frozen)

a small bunch mint leaves, torn from the stem

a small bunch chives, finely chopped

a small bunch dill, broken into fronds

3 large handfuls pea shoots

250g hot smoked trout, roughly broken into chunks

For the dressing

240g natural yoghurt

1 tbsp olive oil

plenty of salt and pepper

1 tbsp freshly squeezed lemon juice

1 tsp creamed horseradish sauce

Boil the potatoes until just tender. Two minutes before the end of their cooking time, add the peas. Once cooked, drain off the water and run the potatoes and peas under cold water until cool to the touch. Drain again.

Next, combine the dressing ingredients and mix well till blended. Taste and season.

Finally, mix together the potatoes, peas, herbs, pea shoots and smoked trout. Drizzle the dressing over and serve straight away.

Swap in ... Smoked salmon instead of hot smoked trout. Replace pea shoots with soft green leaves such as lamb's lettuce, Little Gem lettuce or young watercress. Replace the lemon juice with malt vinegar or the chives with spring onions.

This is the salad you're looking for if you're having a barbecue: the flavours are great with charred chicken or pork. It works well with grilled meaty white fish like hake, swordfish or monkfish. It's also the green salad I relish on its own as a light supper. It's wonderful with a cheese course (and a dressing made simply of half olive oil, half lemon juice). In short, this is my 'Go-to' Salad – the one I want different ways in *every* season.

222 calories per portion
1½ of your five-a-day

'Go-to' Green Salad

Serves 4

2 small round lettuce, broken into leaves

½ quantity Light Caesar Dressing (page 188)

salt and pepper, to taste

30 mint leaves

10 sprigs dill

25 tarragon leaves

30 small basil leaves

½ small red onion, finely diced

finely grated zest of ½ unwaxed lemon

Wash and spin the lettuce leaves dry. When you get to the 'heart' of the lettuce, cut it out. I often just eat it there and then, as it doesn't really belong in this salad because it's too crunchy.

Make up the dressing, taste and season with salt and pepper, then toss the leaves in half the dressing. Add the herbs, diced onion and lemon zest.

Serve with the leaves stacked up and any remaining dressing drizzled over the top.

Swap in.... This is the richest of the dressings I put with this salad, but it's also wonderful with the Balsamic Vinaigrette (page 188), or the Swiss Vinaigrette (page 189). The herbs can be switched around as you wish. If I can ever get hold of any chervil, I add it to this mixture. And sometimes I like to include a bit of avocado as well.

I'm sitting opposite one of my favourite people (an Irish New Yorker called Ultan who somehow seems to know *stuff* about everything from architecture to daffodils, to oysters and beer, to buttons and bows). Over lunch, he starts talking about a salad made from grilled avocado. I now make it once a month because it's the perfect small supper and grilling the avocado gives it a nutty, silky flavour. Even the simplest version of this recipe, with just tomatoes, coriander and lime juice, is sensational.

226 calories per portion
2½ of your five-a-day

Grilled Avocado and Cherry Tomato with lime and coriander

Serves 2

1 whole avocado, ripe but on the firm side

2 limes

230g cherry tomatoes, cut into quarters

1 tsp olive oil

1 small clove fresh garlic, minced

a small handful coriander leaves, torn from the stem

plenty of salt and pepper

1 tsp sesame seeds, toasted in a dry pan until golden

Heat a frying pan until very hot. Slice the avocados in half across the middle and discard the stone, then place them cut face down in the hot pan and cook for 2 minutes. Remove, score the flesh and squeeze the juice of 1 lime over them.

Next, add the cherry tomatoes to the hot pan and swirl them around for 30 seconds until lightly warmed through.

Toss the warm cherry tomatoes in the olive oil with the garlic, juice from the remaining lime, coriander and plenty of salt and pepper.

Top the avocado with the fragrant tomato mixture piled into the hollow and sprinkle the toasted sesame seeds over. Serve warm, with a spoon or a fork as the only implement needed.

Swap in ... Add finely chopped chilli (red and green), a heaped tablespoon of crab meat per avocado half, toasted sunflower seeds, paprika. Use lemon juice instead of lime and basil instead of coriander, finely chopped spring onions instead of garlic. This would also be delicious with the cherry tomatoes and some Lime and Coriander Pesto (page 190). I like having this salad warm, as it releases the flavours beautifully, but you can also just have it all cold if you prefer.

245 calories per portion
3 of your five-a-day

You can actually find the ingredients for this salad all year round, since soya beans are mostly bought frozen. I do, however, prefer this zingy recipe in spring or early summer when the world is wasabi green and bursting into life.

Hot Smoked Salmon, Edamame and Cucumber with a wasabi cream dressing

Serves 2

160g frozen soya beans

1 medium cucumber, washed

100g pink radish, washed, trimmed and sliced into fine circles

160g hot smoked salmon, flaked

¼ tsp poppy seeds

For the wasabi cream dressing

½ tsp wasabi paste

1 tsp tahini paste

2 tbsp full-fat yoghurt

2 tsp rice vinegar

Cook the soya beans according to packet instructions. As a rule, I tend to err on the undercooked side of vegetable-cooking instructions as I like my beans to have texture and bite. Once cooked, drain and run cold water over the beans until they are cool to the touch. Drain and pat dry with kitchen paper.

Cut the cucumber into long ribbons using a potato-peeler, turning the vegetable as you go so that you end up with the seeds in the middle left in your hand. Discard (or eat) the watery middle part.

Next, combine the dressing ingredients in a clean jam jar and give a good shake.

Lightly mix together the beans, cucumber ribbons, radish circles and smoked salmon. Pour the dressing over and scatter the poppy seeds on top before serving. The dressing has a surprising kick to it (which I happen to love), so you may want to let people dress their own salads.

Swap in ... I have also made this salad with a medium sliced avocado instead of the salmon as a vegetarian version and it's completely delicious. The only thing is, you may then want to add some salt at the end, since the salmon is where most of the salt comes from in the original recipe.

This is a classic American diner dish and wonderfully retro. I've seen it as an accompaniment to burgers or steak, as well as a stand-alone salad. It can come loaded with all sorts of extras but the basic recipe is: iceberg lettuce cut into quarters, crispy bacon, blue cheese dressing and chives. Iceberg really shines because it provides the cool, crunchy, neutral backdrop for other fuller flavours.

400 calories per portion
1 of your five-a-day

Iceberg Wedge with Blue Cheese and Bacon

Serves 4

200g pancetta, cut into small cubes

a small, tightly packed head of iceberg lettuce

a small handful chives, finely chopped

70g Danish Blue cheese, crumbled

freshly ground black pepper

For the blue cheese dressing

40g Danish Blue cheese, squashed to a paste with the back of a spoon

30g mayonnaise (I like Hellmann's)

90g sour cream

90g buttermilk

½ tsp Worcestershire sauce

salt and black pepper

Fry the pancetta in a large dry frying pan, making sure to stir once in a while so that the meat is golden on all sides. Set aside once the pancetta is crispy.

Make the blue cheese dressing by combining, first, the cheese paste with the mayonnaise and stirring until it's well blended and there aren't too many lumps.

Next, whip in the sour cream, buttermilk and the Worcestershire sauce. Taste, and season with salt and black pepper.

Cut the bottom off the iceberg, then divide the lettuce into quarters. Drizzle the blue cheese dressing over, then sprinkle with the pancetta, chives and the crumbled blue cheese. Season with black pepper and serve straight away.

Swap in ... I like this salad with either croutons or toasted pecans instead of the pancetta. If you like your blue cheese really strong and salty, replace the Danish Blue with Roquefort.

I was lucky enough to assist an awesome Lebanese food writer from Sydney for a number of years. Apart from all the other wonderful recipes I picked up, Jacque Malouf taught me about proper fattoush, which is a heavenly mixture of crunch, citrus and aromatics – all bundled up in a refreshing salad. Because the cherry tomatoes start to get really red and delicious earlier in the year, this to me is a great spring salad.

222 calories per portion
3 of your five-a-day

Lebanese Fattoush

Serves 4

2 pitta breads, cut in half

2 tsp olive oil

½ medium cucumber, washed under the tap

1 head cos lettuce, washed and roughly chopped

1 small red onion, finely sliced

100g pink radish, finely sliced

1 tbsp sumac

a large bunch parsley leaves, torn from the stalks

150g cherry tomatoes on the vine, cleaned and cut in half through the waist

2 cloves garlic, peeled

For the dressing

2 tbsp red wine vinegar

2 tbsp olive oil

2 tbsp freshly squeezed lemon juice

plenty of salt and black pepper

Preheat the oven to 200°C/400°F/gas mark 6. Brush the pitta bread with the olive oil, place on a baking sheet and bake for 10 minutes until golden and crispy. Set aside.

Meanwhile, whisk together the dressing ingredients in a large bowl until well combined. Taste and season.

Next, cut the cucumber down the middle and run a teaspoon down the core to remove the seeds. Cut the cucumber into cubes and add to the bowl with the dressing, together with the prepared lettuce, red onion, radish, sumac, parsley leaves and tomatoes. Toss to coat.

Finally, rub the garlic over the rough side of the crisp pitta. Break the bread into pieces and add to the fattoush. Give one final toss and serve.

Swap in … It isn't traditionally Lebanese, but you could add strips of grilled lamb, olives and toasted seeds or pine nuts to this salad. You could replace the cherry tomatoes with sunblush or sun-dried ones for a slightly more intense flavour.

In the last year I have become quite obsessed with pickling vegetables. This is the lightest and easiest form of this wondrous technique and requires only 10 minutes. You'll find that the cucumber is softened and imbued with a tangy, sweet flavour that comes from the mixture of the sugar, salt and raspberry vinegar. It's good news for all of you out there who are looking for light, pretty salads that are also low in fat and calories!

160 calories per portion
3 of your five-a-day

Lightly Pickled Beetroot, Cucumber and Feta
with raspberry dressing

Serves 2

240g cucumber, peeled and finely sliced

240g cooked beetroot (look for the type that isn't vac-packed in vinegar)

1 very small red onion, cut into thin rings

40g feta, crumbled

a small handful dill leaves, torn from the stem

freshly ground white pepper

2 tsp olive oil

Raspberry dressing

2 tbsp Raspberry Vinegar (page 192), or shop-bought equivalent

1 tsp caster sugar

½ tsp salt

Mix the raspberry dressing ingredients together in a bowl and stir until the sugar has dissolved.

Add the cucumber slices to the dressing and let them stand for 10 minutes whilst you slice the beetroot very finely. Once the cucumber has had its time, remove it from the bowl with a slotted spoon and set aside.

Add the beetroot slices to the bowl with the sweet and sour dressing and give them a good toss. Allow them to stand for 5 minutes to take on the flavour of the dressing.

Divide the beetroot between two plates and arrange the cucumber slices over the top.

Finally, sprinkle over the red onion, feta, dill and a crunch of white pepper before serving with the olive oil drizzled over the lot.

Swap in … Smoked salmon or gravlax instead of feta. Add capers and have it on the side of a blini with sour cream. You can use Thyme and Tangerine Vinegar (page 193) instead of raspberry, or sherry vinegar if you have neither.

My fella is American. I call him Minnesota. He loves steak and bourbon and smelly cheese . . . and salad. So this recipe is a man's take on his favourite salad, his 'go-to' dinner when he's on his own, or cooking for friends, or for me. All the notes come from Minnesota himself. He was especially adamant about the Mozzarella (see below).

525 calories per portion
1½ of your five-a-day

Minnesota Salad

Serves 2

3 large handfuls mixed baby lettuce leaves (such as red chard, butterhead or rocket), washed and dried

1 small red pepper, sliced into very thin strips

¼ red onion, sliced into very thin strips

200g fresh Mozzarella – use only the really good stuff (if you can only get the white plastic, then you may as well use a goat's cheese, like 150g goat log)

75g roasted red pepper (such as piquillo pepper), very thinly sliced (home-made or store-bought)

100g cured ham (such as prosciutto, Parma or Bayonne – the darker the meat, the better)

For the dressing

4 tsp balsamic vinegar

salt and black pepper

4 tsp olive oil

Crack open a beer or pour a glass of wine whilst you get the salad stuff ready.

Make the dressing in a big bowl by whisking together first the vinegar and a pinch of salt and pepper. Add the oil next and whisk to combine. This way the salt and pepper don't 'sit' on top of the dressing.

Add the lettuce leaves, fresh peppers and red onion to the dressing and toss to coat evenly.

Divide between two plates and add the Mozzarella (or goat's cheese), roasted red peppers and ham slices. Serve right away with a big glass of red wine.

Swap in... As mentioned above, replace the Mozzarella with a slightly smaller quantity of goat's cheese if you can't find good stuff. I also like to use crispy lettuce like Little Gem for this salad when baby lettuce leaves aren't in season. Add avocado and black olives for days of Great Hunger, or when watching a Vikings' game (American football), when a lot of energy is spent fist-pumping and shouting at the telly.

I had my first Panzanella recently. For those of you who haven't heard of it (like me up until last Thursday), it's a scruffy salad of tomatoes and stale bread. Sounds boring? It's *not*. This salad is fresh and filling and stuffed with flavour – all the fs. It's also a great way of using up tomatoes that are about to over-ripen, as well as leftover loaf ends that are hiding in the bread bin.

350 calories per portion
4 of your five-a-day

Panzanella

Serves 6

1.5kg ripe tomatoes on the vine, rinsed under the tap

½ tsp soft brown sugar

sea salt

300g stale sourdough bread, torn into roughly equal chunks

2 tbsp sherry vinegar

2 tbsp freshly squeezed lemon juice

120ml extra-virgin olive oil

1 small garlic clove, smashed and minced to a paste

2 tbsp capers, drained and rinsed under the tap

1 large red onion, very thinly sliced

1 cucumber, peeled, de-seeded and cut into rough chunks

a large handful basil, roughly torn

Roughly chop the tomatoes. Put in a bowl and sprinkle with the sugar as well as a good pinch of salt. Let the tomatoes stand for 20 minutes then add the bread. Stand for a further 10 minutes, so that all the tomato liquid at the bottom of the bowl is absorbed by the bread.

Mix the vinegar with the lemon juice and olive oil. Toss the tomatoes and bread with this dressing, then add the remaining ingredients before serving.

Making this salad slightly ahead of when you want to eat it means that the flavours will have extra time to infuse and mingle, which will only improve the flavour.

Swap in ... I have seen recipes where the Panzanella includes black olives and chopped peppers. I added the sugar because I like the contrast, but it's entirely optional. Spring (and indeed summer) this year have been cold and drab. The good news is that you can also heat this salad up and serve it as a chunky, copious soup called Papa al Pomodoro. Simply heat the tomatoes along with all the other ingredients, apart from the basil and the cucumber, in a large saucepan until softened – about 15 minutes. Once cooked, mush roughly together with a fork, season and serve with basil roughly chopped over the top.

332 calories per portion
1½ of your five-a-day

Serves 4

1 thick slice granary bread

1 tbsp olive oil

salt, to taste

270g cos lettuce, washed
 and roughly torn

8 pickled walnuts, quartered

It's wedding season again (yay!) and I've just come back from two crackers: one in Scotland and one in Norfolk. As I think back on the fun of seeing all my old university pals, I find that it's as much about catching up at the pub over lunch before kick-off as it is about the rest of the day. A Ploughman's Salad is what I would go for every time, with a pint of cold lager and a packet of shrimp cocktail crisps, if the salad versions of this beloved sandwich weren't quite so few and far between. Here's hoping that someone out there starts putting it on the menus!

Ploughman's Salad

30g pickled silver onions,
 cut into halves

200g celery, finely sliced
 on the diagonal

160g ham on the bone (or
 hock if you can find it)

1 large pink apple, cored
 and cut into slices

120g mature Cheddar,
 broken into rough chunks

For the dressing

2 tbsp cider vinegar

2 tsp soft brown sugar

2 tsp English mustard

2 tsp Worcestershire sauce

2 tbsp walnut oil

salt, to taste

Combine all the dressing ingredients in a clean jam jar and give a good shake. The sugar should be completely dissolved before you finish.

Brush the bread with the olive oil, season with salt and place in the toaster until golden.

Toss the cos leaves with half the dressing, then add all the remaining ingredients and drizzle the rest of the dressing over.

Swap in … I really like replacing the apple with halved green grapes in this recipe. I also often eat this salad without the ham for a vegetarian version. You can also replace the toast with toasted walnuts if you want to go gluten-free.

Asparagus herald the arrival of spring and are so delicious when they're brand new that I often just eat them with no accompaniment other than a little olive oil and some salt and pepper ground over the top. For this recipe, I wanted something simple yet festive. This makes a wonderful starter when you're entertaining, or a gorgeous supper for one with scrambled eggs and some crusty bread on the side.

191 calories per portion
2 of your five-a-day

Seared Asparagus with Lemon, Garlic and Toasted Almonds

Serves 2

375g asparagus

1 tbsp olive oil

10g butter

1 small clove garlic, minced

plenty of salt and black pepper

finely grated zest of 1 small unwaxed lemon

20g toasted almond flakes

Using a potato-peeler, peel the base of the asparagus about 5cm from the end, as though you were sharpening a pencil. Coat the prepared asparagus with the oil.

Heat up a large frying pan until it's smoking hot and place the asparagus into it. Cook over a high heat until they are charred around the edges – about 5 minutes.

Remove the asparagus from the pan and take it off the heat. Add the butter and garlic to the warm pan and give a good shake to spread it. Once the butter has melted, drizzle it over the cooked asparagus. Season generously with salt and black pepper, then sprinkle with the lemon zest and almond flakes.

Swap in ... Torn prosciutto pieces, shaved Parmesan, butter or truffle oil instead of olive oil. You can also replace the toasted almond flakes with Hazelnut Pesto (page 191).

This is a great, light salad that reminds me of many wonderful Easters spent in Andalucía over the years with my great friend Bells and her family. There are almond and lemon trees on the farm. Come to think of it, there's even a pink peppercorn tree in front of the house . . . This salad is a mental flight to southern Spain, sitting around the kitchen table with Hugh, Jane and Buzz, Bells and the redheads – feeling sunny and happy.

275 calories per portion
1 of your five-a-day

Smoked Chicken, Watercress and Almond with a garlic cream dressing

Serves 2

2 large handfuls ready-to-use watercress leaves

30g Marcona almonds, roughly chopped

a medium bunch tarragon leaves, torn from the stem

150g smoked chicken breast, cut into strips

a pinch freshly ground pink peppercorns

For the dressing

2 tbsp crème fraîche

2 tsp freshly squeezed lemon juice

½ clove garlic, peeled and minced

salt, to taste

Mix together the dressing ingredients until combined. Season with salt.

Assemble the salad by tossing the watercress with the almonds, tarragon and smoked chicken. Drizzle the dressing over and sprinkle with the peppercorns. Serve immediately, as the watercress will start to wilt.

Swap in ... Adding avocado is fantastic in this salad, especially if you toss it in lemon juice. I also like adding lightly blanched asparagus spears, chunks of cooked chorizo sausages and a little parsley. Fried black pudding is also lovely in this salad and works beautifully with the chicken and tarragon.

305 calories per portion
1 of your five-a-day

Serves 4

4 soft-shell crabs, either fresh or frozen

a round head lettuce, leaves broken off the centre and washed

Danny (my super-duper assistant) had never tried soft-shell crab before we tested this recipe together and his face was a picture when he put it into his mouth! He said to me afterwards that it is the kind of recipe that he could become famous for amongst his pals . . . something along the lines of 'Barbecue over at Danny's – I hope he does those crab thingies.' I know just what he means.

Soft-shell Crab with sweet and sour dipping sauce

1 large carrot, peeled and cut into very thin coins

2 spring onions, finely chopped

small handful of fresh mint leaves

For the tempura

4 tbsp cornflour

500ml vegetable oil

For the dressing

3 tbsp freshly squeezed lime juice

2 tbsp fish sauce

2 large cloves garlic, minced

1cm ginger root, peeled and finely grated

1 stalk lemongrass, finely chopped

3 tsp caster sugar

½ tsp fresh red chilli, finely diced

If the crabs are frozen, give yourself around 2 hours to defrost them in the ambient temperature of your kitchen. Make the dressing when you defrost the crabs. Simply combine all the dressing ingredients in a small bowl and stir with a spoon until the sugar has dissolved.

Heat up the oil for the tempura in a small saucepan. You'll know when it's ready because the oil will start to shimmer. Whether fresh or defrosted, pat the crabs dry with kitchen paper before you dredge them thoroughly with the cornflour.

With the help of a pair of tongs, drop the first crab into the hot oil for 2 minutes each side. It should have a lovely, golden, crispy coat. Remove and drain on a piece of kitchen paper whilst you fry the next one, and so on until all the crabs are cooked.

Next, lay down a bed of lettuce leaves and scatter the carrot, spring onions and mint over it. Cut the fried crabs in half down the middle and add to the salad. Drizzle half the dressing over the salad and reserve the rest for dipping.

When it comes to helping yourself, wrap up half a crab in a lettuce leaf, making sure that you have mint, carrot and spring onion on each leaf. Dunk in the dipping sauce and eat, rolled up like a Peking Duck pancake.

Swap in . . . Add bean shoots, finely sliced water chestnuts or cucumber, but I wouldn't leave out the mint or spring onions.

I'm not wild on rice salads but I do love a wild rice salad (ho ho) . . . The texture of wild rice is so much more robust than most white rice and the flavour is nutty and aromatic. Its dark background lends itself particularly well to spices and pops of colourful ingredients. This is a winner to take on the first picnics of the year and most of the ingredients are probably already in your pantry.

260 calories per portion
1½ of your five-a-day

Spring Store-cupboard Salad of spiced wild rice and garden peas

Serves 6

250g wild rice

5 cardamom pods

3 bay leaves

50g pine nuts

2 medium carrots, peeled and very finely diced

2 tbsp olive oil

2 tsp ground allspice

1 tsp ground coriander

2 tsp cumin seeds

250g garden peas

a medium handful fresh parsley, roughly chopped

1 medium red onion, peeled and very finely diced

freshly squeezed juice of 1 lemon

salt, to taste

Cook the wild rice according to packet instructions, adding the cardamom pods and the bay leaves to the boiling water. Warning: wild rice takes around three times longer to cook than white rice.

Whilst the rice is cooking, heat up a large dry frying pan. Toast the pine nuts over a medium heat until golden brown. Remove and set aside.

Next, add the carrots and 1 tbsp of the olive oil to the warm pan. Cook over a low heat for 5 minutes, until they are slightly coloured and tender when you taste them. Turn the heat off before adding the allspice, ground coriander and cumin seeds. Place the lid back on the pan and set aside to infuse until the rice is ready.

Two minutes before the rice has finished its cooking time, remove the lid and add the peas. Drain and refresh the rice under cold running water until cool to the touch. Remember to remove the bay leaves and cardamom pods.

Add the drained rice and peas to the carrots in the pan and stir. Finally, add the pine nuts, parsley, red onion and the remaining 1 tbsp of olive oil to the rice mixture. Squeeze the lemon juice over, give a last stir and season with plenty of salt. Keeps in the fridge for up to 3 days.

Swap in . . . You could add chopped dried apricots, fried leeks and even little cubes of fried chorizo, or replace the pine nuts with chopped cashew nuts. Top up the wild rice with brown rice, if you fancy.

Today is a cool May day and I'm at home writing and watching the men's French Open final on the telly. As luck would have it, I have some leftover edible flowers from yesterday's testing day with Danny, as well as a pot of fresh mint and some amaranth shoots to play with for my lunch. This salad is delicate and simple. It is perfect as a light side, between courses or to go with cheese. It's also really just a great excuse to eat flowers.

60 calories per portion
1 of your five-a-day

Spring Leaves and Edible Flowers

Serves 1 very geeky tennis fan for lunch

a large handful mixed baby leaves, washed and dried

a small handful baby mint leaves

a small handful edible flowers (such as violas and nasturtiums)

a small handful shoots (such as amaranth, radish or shiso)

For the dressing

1 tbsp Swiss Vinaigrette (page 189) + 1 tsp water

Whisk the Swiss Vinaigrette with the water, until combined.

Put the salad ingredients together and lightly drizzle the dressing over them. Serve straight away, as the flowers and delicate leaves will wilt quickly.

Swap in ... I'm inclined to avoid big flavours or heavy ingredients here, as they would distract from the quiet flavours at play. Saying that, you could serve this salad on the side of a ripe avocado with extra vinaigrette or a soft-in-the-centre baked egg with cream. You could add a small amount of finely chopped chives to the salad itself. If you're a fan of sashimi, try this salad on the side of raw sea bass or tuna slices, dipped in wasabi and soy sauce.

Combining veal liver with a lemon sauce is a dish that is often found in French brasseries. It's the most fabulous pairing you can imagine. Here, again, the lemon hit helps to cut through the richness of the sweetbreads and the flavour of the peas and capers enhances its sweetness.

350 calories per portion
1½ of your five-a-day

Sweetbreads, Peas, Parsley and Capers

Serves 4

2 Little Gem lettuces, leaves broken from the heart and washed

2 large handfuls pea shoots

a small handful flat-leaf parsley leaves

340g garden peas, blanched and refreshed in cold water

450g prepared lamb sweetbreads (the freshest possible) – do yourself a favour and get the butcher to prepare them

1 tbsp vegetable oil

30g butter

2 tbsp small capers, drained of brine

For the lemon shallot vinaigrette

2 shallots, finely diced

6 tbsp freshly squeezed lemon juice

2 tsp walnut oil

2 tsp Dijon mustard

plenty of salt and pepper

To make the dressing, whisk all the ingredients until combined.

Put the lettuce, pea shoots, parsley and peas in a large bowl and toss with the dressing.

Wash the sweetbreads under the cold tap and pat dry. Break them up into small pieces along the natural lines and remove any visible fat. You want pieces of roughly the same size so that they will cook evenly.

Next, heat the vegetable oil in a large frying pan until hot and add the sweetbread pieces. Fry for 2 minutes, then flip them all over, add the butter and cook for a further 2 minutes. Remove with a slotted spoon and set aside on kitchen paper.

Finally, add the capers to the hot pan then switch off the heat. They will sizzle furiously for a couple of minutes. When the sizzling has died down they are ready to use.

Add the sweetbreads to the salad and serve immediately, sprinkling the capers over at the end.

Swap in ... Baby leaf lettuce instead of Little Gem, veal sweetbreads instead of lamb. The main thing is to honour the balance between the rich, buttery sweetbreads and the sharp lemon and capers ... Oh, and to be sure to keep it French. *Mais oui!*

The clue is in the title! This recipe was inspired by a trip to New York, where I came across potato salads with literally *everything* in them. And boy, were they good! The pastrami and dill pickles are reminiscent of the wonderful Jewish delis that pepper the lower East Side. I like serving this salad at picnics or barbecues, where everyone dives in and helps themselves. I tend to have a simple green salad (such as 'Go-to' Green Salad, page 14) alongside too.

307 calories per portion
½ of your five-a-day

Whopping Potato Salad

Serves 4

500g new potatoes (Charlotte or other waxy varieties)

2 large free-range eggs

30g wholegrain mustard

50g mayonnaise (I prefer Hellmann's)

½ tsp malt vinegar

salt and pepper, to taste

4 spring onions, finely chopped

2 sticks celery, finely chopped

150g thinly sliced pastrami, roughly chopped

70g large sweet pickled gherkins, finely chopped

a small bunch dill leaves, torn from the stem

Boil the potatoes until just tender. Add the eggs to the pan around 8 minutes before the end of the potatoes' cooking time.

Drain the potatoes and eggs, then run the eggs under cold water to cool. Peel the eggs and set them aside.

Mix the mustard with the mayonnaise and vinegar. Taste and season.

Cut the cooled potatoes into halves or quarters, depending on how big they are, then toss to coat in the mayonnaise mixture.

Roughly chop the eggs and add to the mixture, along with the spring onions, celery, pastrami, pickled gherkins and dill. Refrigerate until needed and serve at room temperature.

Swap in ... You could add peas, ham hock pieces (to replace the pastrami), toasted pumpkin seeds, finely diced red onion or chives.

465 calories per portion
2½ of your five-a-day

Serves 6

4 medium chicken breasts, skinless

1 tbsp olive oil

2 heads cos lettuce, leaves broken from the heart and washed

I realize that mango isn't ever really seasonal in Britain, but it's just so darn delicious with Coronation Chicken that I decided to put it in anyway. As for this Coronation sauce recipe, it comes straight from my Auntie Sarah's loved and worn book of handwritten recipes. It's a bit more fiddly than just bunging together a paste and some mayonnaise, but it's the real thing and is really worth the extra effort.

Coronation Chicken with cos lettuce and mango

1 whole mango, peeled, pitted and cut into long thin strips

1 red onion, finely diced

1 red pepper, de-seeded and cut into long thin strips

15g slivered almond flakes, lightly toasted in a dry frying pan

For the Coronation dressing

2 tbsp vegetable oil

1 onion, peeled and very finely diced

2 tsp medium Madras curry powder (I like Bart's)

1 heaped tbsp tomato purée

150ml red wine (anything you would drink)

freshly squeezed juice of 1 lemon

2 bay leaves

2 tbsp mango chutney

3 tbsp mayonnaise (I like Hellmann's)

150ml plain yoghurt

a pinch salt

To make the Coronation dressing, heat the oil in a small saucepan and add the onion. Cook over a medium heat for 4 minutes before adding the curry powder. Cook for a further 2 minutes. Next, add the tomato purée, wine, lemon juice and bay leaves. Bring to the boil and simmer, uncovered, for 6 minutes. Stir in the mango chutney.

Strain through a sieve and cool. Press down on the mesh of the sieve with the back of a spoon to really get *everything*. Once cool, add the mayonnaise and yoghurt, then season to taste. You can expect to add a fair bit of salt to bring it up to the right seasoning.

Next, heat a chargrill frying pan. Butterfly each chicken breast by cutting into the thick part of the meat and opening it out like a book. Place each butterflied chicken breast between two sheets of cling film and gently bash it out with a meat mallet or a rolling pin. You want the meat to be around 1 cm thick and twice its original surface area.

Rub the chicken breasts in olive oil and place one into the hot pan. Cook for 4 minutes each side, then set aside and repeat with the next breast. Cut into strips. Make a bed with the cos lettuce leaves and pile on the chicken, mango, onion, red pepper and a generous helping of the dressing. Scatter the toasted almonds over before serving.

Swap in ... Apricot jam instead of mango chutney, tinned peaches or apricots (sliced) instead of the mango, Little Gem lettuce instead of cos, a little red chilli instead of the red pepper.

Although I love cooked or preserved rhubarb, I always find that some of the 'rhubarb-ness' gets lost in the process . . . So this is a sort of rhubarb ceviche, if you like. The idea is very simply that the sugar and lemon juice 'cook' the raw rhubarb just enough to soften it whilst it stands. It's funny the flavours that you have never detected before that you get from the familiar stalks when it's semi-raw. I taste apples . . . what about you?

116 calories per portion
2 of your five-a-day

Rhubarb, Raspberry and Crystallized Ginger *for Nina*

Serves 4

400g fresh rhubarb, rinsed under the tap

50g caster sugar

2 tbsp freshly squeezed lemon juice

200g fresh raspberries, rinsed under the tap

50g crystallized ginger, roughly chopped

Using a sharp knife, slice the rhubarb as finely as you can. The finer it's sliced, the more flavour you will extract.

Place the rhubarb slices in a bowl with the caster sugar and lemon juice. Set aside for 2 hours in the ambient temperature of the kitchen to marinate and 'cook'.

Toss the fruit occasionally. You can expect a pool of pink juice to form at the bottom of the bowl.

Once the rhubarb has sat out, add the raspberries and the crystallized ginger. Allow to sit for a further 30 minutes to macerate before serving.

This is delicious on its own but also with thick vanilla yoghurt and shortbread biscuits.

Swap in ... $\frac{1}{4}$ tsp rosewater and some roughly chopped Turkish delight instead of the crystallized ginger. You could also add lightly toasted, chopped pistachios. Serve with vanilla custard, vanilla or ginger ice cream.

I love the idea of adding cucumber to fruit salads, especially with the combination of mint and Pimm's light syrup here. This is an ideal dessert for outdoor entertaining when the weather is warm enough to linger at the lunch or dinner table. When shopping for the ingredients, you're looking for fruits that are ripe but firm. If they're too soft, they will lose their texture in the salad.

173 calories per portion
3 of your five-a-day

Pimm's Fruit Salad

Serves 6

400g strawberries, hulled and rinsed under the tap

½ large cucumber, peeled

2 English apples (such as Gala)

½ lemon

2 oranges

2 peaches

a small bunch mint leaves, roughly chopped

For the Pimm's syrup

200ml Pimm's

70g caster sugar

To make the syrup, heat the Pimm's with the sugar in a small saucepan over a medium heat. Simmer for 4 minutes, or until the liquid has reduced by half. Remove from the heat. Refrigerate until cold.

Whilst the syrup cools, halve or quarter the strawberries and toss them into a bowl. Chop the cucumber into 1cm cubes, avoiding the seeds in the centre. Add to the bowl with the strawberries.

Core the apples. Chop into cubes roughly the same size as the cucumber before adding to the rest of the fruit. Stone and slice the peaches. Squeeze the half lemon over the fruit and toss to combine.

Using a knife, slice the peel off the oranges, going from 'north' to 'south'. Slice the segments out from the centre, add to the rest of the fruit and squeeze over any remaining juice.

Pour the Pimm's syrup over the fruit and add the mint leaves. Serve at room temperature.

Swap in ... You could add raspberries, pears, apricots or blackcurrants.

Summer

545 calories per portion
1½ of your five-a-day

Serves 4

150g glass noodles

2 x 200g sirloin steaks, all
visible fat removed

2 tsp vegetable oil

salt, to taste

Whilst I'm sitting at my desk here in London, Minnesota is in Thailand on a work trip. He's been sending me pictures of the food so that I can imagine what it all tastes like. I dreamt up this salad as a means of mentally travelling to Bangkok on this damp June day. I make this recipe with European basil because Thai basil is difficult to find, but if you can keep to the authentic ingredient, so much the better . . .

Thai Beef and Basil
with glass noodles

3 Little Gem lettuces, leaves
torn from the heart and
washed

½ cucumber, halved
lengthways, cored with a
teaspoon and thinly sliced

1 red onion, halved and cut
into thin strips

a large handful fresh basil
leaves, roughly torn

60g salted cashew nuts,
toasted in a frying pan
and roughly chopped

For the dressing

3 tbsp freshly squeezed
lime juice

3 tbsp palm sugar or soft
brown sugar

2 tbsp fish sauce

1 tbsp dark soy sauce

2 tbsp sesame oil + 1 tsp
for the noodles

2 tsp fresh ginger, finely
grated

2 tsp garlic, finely grated

2 long, fresh red chillies,
halved, de-seeded and
finely chopped

Whisk together all the ingredients for the dressing in a medium-sized bowl.

Cook the noodles according to packet instructions, then drain and toss in 1 tsp sesame oil to prevent them from sticking. Using a pair of scissors, chop into the noodles to break up the long, thin strands.

Heat up a chargrill frying pan over a high heat. Rub the oil into the meat until the steaks are glistening all over.

When the pan is really hot, fry the steaks. I like mine to be rare so I give it about 2 minutes per side, but if you like yours more well done, then leave it on for longer. Once cooked, season with salt and set aside on a plate to rest.

Combine all the salad ingredients except the toasted nuts in a big bowl and pour the dressing over. Toss to coat evenly.

Once the steaks have had 5 minutes' resting time, slice them into strips and add to the salad with the toasted cashews. Serve straight away.

Swap in ... You could replace the Little Gem lettuce with pak choi, substitute either peanuts or sesame seeds for the cashews, replace the beef with pork tenderloin or fried tofu for a vegetarian version. Deep-fried onions would be delicious here too.

Whether they're cut into thin coins or finely sliced ribbons, raw courgettes are one of my top fave salad ingredients. When the yellow ones start appearing in early summer I like dreaming up recipes that include them. This is a simple, fresh, light salad that is perfect on its own with a hunk of bread dipped in olive oil, or on the side of a plate of chargrilled chicken or fish.

195 calories per portion
1 of your five-a-day

Yellow and Green Courgettes with Feta, Mint and Almonds

Serves 4

1 tbsp olive oil

freshly squeezed juice and zest of 1 unwaxed lemon

salt, to taste

3 medium green and yellow courgettes, topped and tailed

140g feta, crumbled

¼ tsp pink peppercorns, crushed in a mortar and pestle

a small handful mint leaves, roughly torn

30g flaked almonds, lightly toasted in a dry pan until golden

Combine the olive oil with the lemon juice in a clean jar and shake until blended. Season with a little salt.

Using a mandoline or a very sharp knife, slice the courgettes into thin coins and toss them in the dressing to coat them. You can also peel the courgettes lengthways into ribbons, for a slightly different version of this salad. Allow to stand for 10 minutes to 'cook' the courgettes and soften them.

Finally add the feta, crushed peppercorns, lemon zest, mint and almonds and toss once more to combine. Serve at room temperature.

Swap in ... Chopped hazelnuts instead of almonds, white pepper instead of pink peppercorns, shreds of Serrano ham, torn Mozzarella and basil instead of feta and mint.

555 calories per portion
(**339** calories minus aioli)
1 of your five-a-day

Serves 4

3 tbsp olive oil + 2 tsp extra
for frying

500g new potatoes (such
as Charlotte)

It's asparagus season so I'm going a little crazy and making everything asparagus at the moment. When asparagus are very fine, I like eating them raw, as in this salad. If you can't find the very thin type, simply cut the thicker variety lengthways into quarters or halves. The aioli is delicious as a dollop on the scallops and the new potatoes.

Scallops, Asparagus and Spinach
with rosemary-roasted new potatoes and saffron aioli

salt and black pepper

2 tbsp rosemary leaves,
bruised with the back of
a knife

1 tbsp freshly squeezed
lemon juice

12 scallops

3 large handfuls baby
spinach leaves, rinsed
and drained

200g fine asparagus,
rinsed under the tap

a small handful flat-leaf
parsley leaves, torn from
the stem

For the saffron aioli

a large pinch saffron

1 tbsp freshly squeezed
lemon juice

2 cloves garlic, minced

8 tbsp mayonnaise (I like
Hellmann's)

Preheat the oven to 200°C/400°F/gas mark 6.

Soak the saffron in 1 tbsp lemon juice and set aside for later.

Heat 2 tbsp of olive oil in a large saucepan and add the new potatoes. Cook over a high heat until their skins are golden. Transfer the potatoes to an ovenproof dish. Crunch over some salt and a little pepper. Add the rosemary and cover in foil before cooking in the middle of the hot oven for 15 minutes. Remove from the oven and set aside to cool down. Discard the rosemary.

Knock up the lemon vinaigrette by whisking together the remaining 1 tbsp olive oil with 1 tbsp of lemon juice. Season with salt. To make the aioli, combine the saffron, lemon juice in which it has been steeping, minced garlic and mayonnaise.

Fry the scallops in 2 tsp of oil in the frying pan from earlier. I like mine crispy on the outside and underdone in the middle, so I tend to cook them over a very high heat for only a minute or two on each side.

To assemble the salad, toss the spinach, fine asparagus and parsley in a large bowl with the lemon vinaigrette. Divide between four plates and add the scallops and new potatoes. Serve with the aioli on the side.

Swap in ... Use toasted potato farls (cut into strips) instead of roast potatoes if you want to cut down the cooking time.

Aubergines are downright scary if you don't know how to handle them, but this easy fritter recipe will take away all the fear. This idea came from lunch in an Italian restaurant in Chicago, where all five of us ordered a different salad as a means of helping me with the research for this book! The aubergine salad won by a mile. This one's for Lance, Snow, Barb and Minnesota.

280 calories per portion
2½ of your five-a-day

Beefsteak Tomatoes with Aubergine Fritters

Serves 6

2 medium aubergines

plenty of salt

2 large free-range eggs

a small bunch oregano leaves, torn from the stem and very finely shredded

125g breadcrumbs – the finer and cheaper, the better

6 tbsp vegetable oil

3 large beefsteak tomatoes

3 large handfuls rocket

For the dressing

3 tbsp Balsamic Glaze (shop-bought, or see page 186)

freshly squeezed juice of ½ lemon

Cut the aubergines into very thin coins roughly ½ cm thick. I tend to start about 2cm from each end, so that the circles aren't too small.

Once you have all the aubergine circles laid out on a tray, sprinkle them lightly with salt and let them stand for 20 minutes. Water will rise up from the vegetable like little beads of sweat. Dab with kitchen paper.

Next, beat the eggs in a shallow bowl with half the oregano leaves. Tip the breadcrumbs on to a plate. Dip the aubergine slices first into the egg, then into the breadcrumbs, making sure to coat both sides. Repeat this process until all the slices are 'egg-and-breadcrumbed'.

Meanwhile, heat up a large frying pan with some of the vegetable oil until hot. Fry the aubergine slices for 3 minutes on each side, fitting as many slices into the pan as you can without crowding it, then set aside on kitchen paper once cooked. Repeat with new oil for the next batch and so on until they're all cooked.

Once all the aubergine slices are cooked, assemble the salad by alternating slices of tomato with aubergine. Scatter the rocket liberally over the top and drizzle the Balsamic Glaze over. Finally, sprinkle with the last of the oregano and squeeze a little lemon juice over the aubergine slices. Serve warm.

Swap in … Feta or Mozzarella would be a lovely addition. Add in some mint or basil with the rocket and take out the oregano.

Broad beans always remind me of my late grandmother, Margaret. She was famously *not* a cook (and many funny stories over the years attest to this!), but at a handful of things, she was outstanding. Being a keen gardener meant that her vegetables were fresh and wonderful. Although she had a particular talent for raspberries and gooseberries, it was her broad beans for which she really shone.

412 calories per portion
2½ of your five-a-day

Broad Beans, Peas, Pancetta and Mint

Serves 2

220g broad beans

190g garden peas

140g pancetta cubes

2 tbsp extra-virgin olive oil

freshly squeezed juice and
zest of 1 unwaxed lemon

salt and freshly ground
black pepper

a handful mint leaves, torn
from the stems

100g fresh ricotta

Cook the broad beans in a saucepan of boiling water until tender – roughly 6 minutes. I like mine to be ever so slightly underdone. Add the peas for the last 2 minutes' cooking. Drain through a colander and sit under cold, running water until the beans are cool inside when tasted. Drain again.

Whilst the beans and peas are cooking, heat a dry frying pan until hot then add the pancetta. Fry until golden and crispy, then use a slotted spoon to transfer to a plate covered with kitchen paper.

Mix together the olive oil, lemon juice and plenty of salt and black pepper.

Pour the dressing over the beans and peas before adding the cooked pancetta and mint. Dot the ricotta on at the last minute and sprinkle the lemon zest over.

Swap in... For a vegetarian version you could replace the pancetta with chopped sunblush tomatoes and toasted pine nuts, or add in dill, a little garlic, basil or chives.

I made this up the other day when Minnesota and I wanted to take a small picnic down to the edge of the Seine. We bought the baguette sandwiches (I always get *jambon-beurre*) and the beers, but a fresh, light salad that could keep for the time it takes to get there was missing. This one is refreshing, light and perfect for summer lunches. The idea came to me because of a delicious cold cucumber soup that my stepmother Sophie makes at this time of year, which is spiked with a little garlic and lots of mint.

37 calories per portion
2 of your five-a-day

Cucumber and Yoghurt
with mint, dill and chives

Serves 4 as a side salad

2 whole cucumbers, peeled, seeds removed with a teaspoon

120g pot natural yoghurt (I like to use probiotic if I can)

plenty of salt and black pepper

a small handful mint leaves

a small handful dill fronds

a small handful chives, finely chopped

Chop the prepared cucumber into rough chunks.

Mix the cucumber chunks with the yoghurt and season with salt and pepper. Scatter the herbs over just before serving.

Swap in ... You can also add chopped celery or finely cut fennel to this salad if you like. A tiny splash of malt vinegar works well in this salad too if you like a little extra acidity.

This is a fruit salad – suspended in elderflower jelly. There is literally no smell or taste that conjures up English summer to me like elderflower. This dessert is refreshing for dinner or summer lunches and is positively cinch-ish to knock up in 10 minutes the day before.

237 calories per portion
1 of your five-a-day

Elderflower and Summer Berry Jelly

Serves 6

800ml water

500ml good-quality elderflower cordial (I like the Belvoir's organic range)

8 gelatine leaves

600g mixed berries (strawberries, blackberries, raspberries), washed and hulled

Mix together the water and elderflower cordial in a large bowl.

Scoop out 2 ladlefuls of the mixture into a small saucepan and heat. When the liquid is hot but still cool enough for you to be able to put your finger in comfortably for a few seconds, add the gelatine leaves. Remove from the heat and stir with a spoon until dissolved – this can take a few minutes.

When all the gelatine has dissolved, add the warm mixture to the rest and stir again.

Divide the berries between six glasses and pour the elderflower mixture over them.

Refrigerate overnight and serve cold.

TIP: Gelatine is such a funny ingredient. The key to a really lovely jelly is to make sure that it's soft, as opposed to rubbery. This comes from using the very minimum amount of gelatine and chilling it for longer than just a few hours.

Swap in ... I love the summer berry combination, but you could swap in any soft fruit you fancy, like peach, pear, pomegranate or even ripe plums. The only fruit that won't work here, because their natural acidity prevents the jelly from setting, are kiwis and pineapple.

I often forget about bresaola . . . yet it's such a wonderful ingredient. This simple salad is a lively, fresh affair that's ready in minutes. If you're travelling, plonk this salad inside a ciabatta roll and drizzle over a little extra olive oil for a really wonderful sandwich.

255 calories per portion
3 of your five-a-day

Fennel, Pear, Pecorino and Celery
with bresaola and poppy seeds

Serves 2

1 small fennel bulb

1 small conference pear, cut in half and cored

2 celery stalks with green tops

1 tsp poppy seeds

45g bresaola slices (around 10), roughly torn

30g Pecorino, thinly shaved

For the dressing

2 tsp freshly squeezed lemon juice

1 tbsp olive oil

Whisk the lemon juice and olive oil together to make the dressing.

Cut the fennel bulb in half lengthways. Using a mandoline or an extremely sharp knife, shave the halved fennel into very thin strips. Tip them into a large mixing bowl.

Next cut the pear into thin strips along its length. Add the pear to the fennel shavings and pour the prepared lemon dressing over. Toss to coat evenly.

Slice the celery stalk finely, then roughly chop the leaves at the top and add them to the bowl with the pear and fennel. Add the poppy seeds.

Add the bresaola and the Pecorino just before serving, then give it all one final toss.

Swap in . . . I really like this salad with the Light Caesar Dressing (page 188). It's also lovely with grapes cut in half instead of pear. Add toasted pecans and pomegranates for a more copious, autumn version.

The most wonderful thing happens to goat's cheese when it's encased in a shell of thin, crispy pastry: it melts and mellows and surrenders any sourness it may once have had. This deeply French combination is perfect with a slightly bitter leaf and a hint of walnuts. You could also make smaller versions of these parcels and serve them as canapés.

707 calories per portion
1 of your five-a-day

Goat's Cheese and Honey Parcels
with green beans

Serves 6 (3 parcels each)

400g fine haricot beans, topped and tailed

9 sheets filo pastry

4 tbsp vegetable oil

350g mild goat's cheese (such as goat log), cut into 18 round slices

18 x ½ tsp set honey (I like a floral one like lavender or orange blossom)

2 tbsp thyme leaves, torn from the stem

200g lardons, chopped into very small dice

4 large handfuls oak leaf lettuce or mixed baby leaf lettuce, washed and dried

1 banana shallot, finely diced

For the dressing

1 tbsp red wine vinegar

1 tbsp walnut oil

1 tsp Dijon mustard

Blanch the haricot beans in boiling water and once the water boils again drain and rinse them in very cold water until they are cold to the touch. They should be a little crunchy. Drain and set aside.

To make the parcels, cut the filo sheets in half lengthways then brush a little of the oil over the first sheet of filo on both sides. Next, place a cheese round somewhere in the middle of each sheet and top it with ½ tsp honey and a pinch thyme. Fold the cheese up like a present, over and over itself, tucking in the ends as you go so that you don't wind up with any 'open ends'. Don't worry that it's not glued tight shut at this point as the melted cheese and honey will seal it later. Once you've made up all the parcels, set them aside.

Fry the lardons in a large dry frying pan. Once golden and cooked, remove them from the pan with a slotted spoon and drip-dry them on kitchen paper.

Without tipping the excess fat out of the pan, fry the filo cheese parcels in the lardon pan for 4 minutes on each side, or until they turn golden.

Blend the dressing ingredients together in a clean jam jar and give a good shake. Assemble the salad leaves, shallot, lardons and beans in a large mixing bowl and toss with the dressing. Taste and season before adding the hot parcels and serving.

Swap in … For a vegetarian version I like to replace the lardons with 120g walnuts, which I toast lightly in the frying pan until golden.

Although I love salads with unusual ingredients and combinations of flavours, I also like solid classic salads like Greek Salad. In the summer, more than ever, I like to have a bigger lunch and a lighter supper. This is exactly the kind of salad that would fit the bill for a late lunch and keep me going for the rest of the day. Lamb is the meat that reminds me of Greece the most and the leg steak, which is the cut used here, is fantastic for the barbecue or the grill, as it has no bone or extra fat.

380 calories per portion
3 of your five-a-day

Greek Salad with Lamb

Serves 2

300g lamb leg steaks, trimmed of any fat

1 tsp olive oil

½ cucumber, peeled, sliced lengthways, seeds removed with a teaspoon, then roughly chopped

250g cherry tomatoes (on the vine if possible), washed and roughly chopped

1 small red onion, finely sliced

50g pitted black olives

2 tsp oregano leaves

salt and pepper, to taste

a small handful Greek basil

For the dressing

1 tbsp olive oil

1 tbsp red wine vinegar

salt and pepper, to taste

Heat a frying pan or barbecue grill. Rub the lamb steaks with 1 tsp of olive oil and, once the pan or grill is really hot, add the lamb and cook over a high heat for 2 minutes on each side. This will give you a pink centre and browned edges. Season the meat then set it aside whilst you put together the rest of the salad.

Make the dressing by combining the ingredients in a clean jam jar and giving a good shake.

Toss the cucumber, tomatoes, red onion, olives and oregano in the dressing. Season with salt and pepper.

Cut the lamb into slices and add to the salad along with the basil before serving.

Swap in ... Substitute the classic feta cheese for the lamb. You could add any number of herbs, including mint or parsley. I like this salad with pieces of toasted pitta bread too.

683 calories per portion
3 of your five-a-day

Serves 4

For the koftas

100g pine nuts, toasted

3 large cloves garlic

It's the first time that I'm meeting any of Minnesota's friends and I thought I'd make this salad for a casual, late lunch. There's quite a bit of cooking involved, but it's easy to do most of the preparation ahead. Plus there's something so nice about chopping and preparing our lunch on this bright Saturday morning, listening to a podcast and sipping on a beer.

Lamb and Saffron Koftas and Sautéed Aubergine
with a mint and yoghurt dressing

500g lamb mince

1 tsp clear honey

3 tbsp thyme leaves, torn from the stems

90g harissa

½ tsp salt

For the sautéed aubergine and red onion salad

1 tbsp olive oil

800g aubergine (roughly 1 huge one), cut into 2.5cm cubes

½ large red onion

a large bunch parsley, roughly chopped

For the mint yoghurt dressing

1 tbsp olive oil

250g Greek yoghurt

2 tbsp freshly squeezed lemon juice

a large bunch mint, finely chopped

Preheat the oven to 160°C/325°F/gas mark 3.

Whizz up the toasted pine nuts and the garlic in the bowl of a food processor until they are coarsely ground. Next add the lamb, honey, thyme, harissa and salt. Form the koftas in your hand so that they are roughly the size of ping-pong balls.

Heat half the olive oil in a large frying pan over a high heat and fry half the aubergine cubes for 8–10 minutes, making sure that they are not crowded in the pan. Remove the aubergine from the pan and set aside, then repeat the process with the other half of the oil and aubergine.

Next, place the fried aubergine in the oven on a baking tray to finish cooking whilst you fry the lamb koftas. To cook the koftas, simply fry them in a dry, non-stick pan for around 5 minutes per batch, making sure to turn them occasionally. Once fried, add them to the aubergine tray in the oven whilst you make the mint and yoghurt dressing.

Combine the olive oil with the yoghurt, then add the lemon juice. Finish by adding the finely chopped mint and stirring to combine. Serve the aubergine and lamb koftas tossed together with the red onion slices, chopped parsley and a dollop of the yoghurt dressing on top.

Swap in ... Replace the lamb koftas with roasted potatoes or chunks of feta coated in harissa for a vegetarian version.

My favourite food writer is a chef called David Tanis. In his second book, *The Heart of the Artichoke*, he too has a light salad of melon and mint, with a twist of lime. I like it at room temperature when the melon smell is so strong it fills the room; and it's also lovely when it's been in the freezer for 15 minutes to chill right down. The appeal of this salad for me is in its outrageous simplicity. And lime makes melon a million times *more melon*.

82 calories per portion
2 of your five-a-day

Lime, Melon and Mint

Serves 2

1 whole Cantaloupe melon, cut into either squares or balls

1 juicy unwaxed lime

10 little mint leaves

It's an old-fashioned tool, but I do love a melon-baller. If you don't have one, chances are that you might have a set of teaspoon measures that are round enough to fake it. In any case, just aim to make the melon balls or cubes roughly the same size.

Squeeze the lime over the melon and give a brief toss to coat.

Just before serving, scatter the mint leaves over.

Swap in ... Frankly, I wouldn't mess with the ingredients here, but I DEFINITELY do like blitzing this together in a blender with lots of ice, some sugar and a slug of tequila to make a variation on the classic, which I like to call Melon Margarita.

I could eat Mozzarella anytime, anywhere – no hunger needed. I just *adore* the stuff. Using peaches in salads is something I discovered over in Australia about eight years ago. The classic combination there is peach and prosciutto, which is also delicious. Use good-quality Mozzarella (buffalo is head and shoulders above the rest) and ripe peaches. If you're looking for a summer lunch, knocked up in 10 minutes to have with a hunk of ciabatta and a glass of crisp white wine, this is *it*.

330 calories per portion
2 of your five-a-day

Peach and Mozzarella
with sweet chilli and tomato glaze

Serves 2

3 ripe peaches, washed, stoned and roughly chopped

150g Mozzarella ball, torn apart with your hands

a handful basil, roughly torn

1 tbsp Sweet Chilli and Tomato Glaze (page 187) or sweet chilli sauce

1 tsp olive oil

salt and black pepper, to taste

Put the peaches and Mozzarella on a large plate. Scatter the basil over, then drizzle first the glaze then the olive oil over everything. Season with a little salt and black pepper before serving.

Swap in ... Toasted pecans, a little rocket, the famous prosciutto mentioned in the introduction. You can use Balsamic Glaze (shop-bought, or see page 186) instead of the Sweet Chilli and Tomato one ... I've made this with barbecued Halloumi before and that works well too. Sometimes I add in chunks of lightly toasted ciabatta that have been soaked in a little olive oil and salt.

When they're at their ripest, sharp-sweet, orange best, peaches and apricots are two of my favourite fruits. The best British passion fruit I have had came from Jersey, of all places. Whether you have this salad as a summer breakfast (as I just did this morning), or as dessert, this quick-to-make fruit salad is a winner. For visual reasons, I seek out the pinkest possible peaches I can find to contrast with the apricots. Any kind of edible flowers you can lay your hands on provide a really lovely finishing touch.

110 calories per portion
3½ of your five-a-day

Peach, Passion Fruit and Apricot
with nasturtiums

Serves 4

600g ripe peaches, washed and cut into segments

400g ripe apricots, cut into quarters

4 passion fruit, flesh scooped out with a spoon

a handful nasturtiums for decoration

Combine the fruit in a medium-sized, shallow bowl and scatter the flowers over before serving.

Swap in ... Mango, strawberries, raspberries, pineapple, pomegranate – any fruit that is either yellow, orange or red will look and taste fantastic.

I get a Caesar Salad craving about three times a year – mostly in the summer. Roasting the chicken here ensures that the meat is tender and full of flavour. Also, my version of the dressing is much lighter than the original one made from raw egg yolks. The simple reason for that is that I'm not a fan of slimy salads. There, I said it.

566 calories per portion
2 of your five-a-day

Roast Chicken Caesar Salad
with quails' eggs

Serves 6

50g butter

2 cloves garlic, minced

1 tbsp thyme leaves

freshly cracked black pepper

1 large (2.5kg) free-range chicken

1 x Light Caesar Dressing (page 188)

12 quails' eggs

1 ciabatta roll, cut into slices 1cm wide, brushed with 2 tbsp olive oil

a pinch celery salt

4 Little Gem lettuces, leaves torn from the heart and washed

120g pitted black olives

3 celery stalks, washed and finely chopped

30g Parmesan, shaved into thin strips

Preheat the oven to 190°C/375°F/gas mark 5.

Beat the butter with a wooden spoon and add the garlic and thyme. It's ready when the mixture looks like a paste. Season well with pepper. Rub the paste under the skin of the chicken, concentrating on the breast section and the top of the thighs. Place the prepared chicken in the middle of the hot oven and cook for 1 hour, basting occasionally.

Meanwhile, make up the Caesar dressing. Cook the quails' eggs in boiling water for 2 minutes. Once cooked, run them under cold water until they are cold to the touch. Drain them, then peel. There is a knack to peeling quails' eggs: roll them on a board first and you'll find that the shell comes off easier (and sometimes in one long, satisfying strip).

Once the chicken has had 40 minutes' cooking, pop the ciabatta on an oven tray and into the hot oven for the final 20 minutes of cooking.

Once the chicken is cooked, let it rest for 10 minutes. Cut all the meat from the carcass and toss it in the cooking juices. Season with celery salt.

Dress the prepared lettuce leaves with half the dressing. Next, add the prepared eggs, olives, celery and ciabatta to the lettuce. Add the Parmesan and a good crunch of black pepper. Drizzle the remaining dressing over before serving.

Swap in ... Avocado instead of chicken. You could also add bacon or toasted seeds, such as pumpkin or sunflower, to replace the croutons for a gluten-free version.

This is a great salad to go for if you're feeling adventurous and want to experiment with new leaf or shoot varieties. There are more ideas of which ones at the end of the recipe. I also often have a small bowl of steamed rice on the side, upon which I dump the odd piece of wasabi-soaked fish or fennel.

405 calories per portion
4 of your five-a-day

Seared Tuna, Fennel, Avocado and Pink Grapefruit with wasabi honey dressing

Serves 2

1 large fennel bulb, very finely sliced

1 small pink grapefruit

1 tsp vegetable oil

2 thick raw tuna steaks

1 tsp dark soy sauce

8 radishes, finely sliced

2 small shallots, cut into fine slices

a few large shiso leaves

1 small avocado, finely diced

For the dressing

2 tbsp freshly squeezed lime juice

2 tsp wasabi paste

2 tsp Chinese rice vinegar

2 tsp clear honey

2 tsp sesame oil

Assemble the dressing ingredients in a large bowl. Add the fennel and toss to coat, then set aside.

With the help of a serrated knife, cut the peel off the grapefruit taking care to also remove the bitter white pith as well. Slice the segments out, discarding the centre, and set aside.

Next, heat a frying pan with the vegetable oil until very hot. Sear the tuna steaks for 30 seconds on each side. Pour the soy sauce over them and stand for 5 minutes, then cut them into strips.

To assemble the salad, mix the fennel with the radish and shallots. Scatter pink grapefruit slices, leaves and avocado over. Finally, top with the tuna slices and serve.

Swap in ... Add toasted sesame seeds. Replace the pink grapefruit with tangerine. You could use swordfish or salmon instead of tuna. As for the leaves, I suggest using sharp, aromatic leaf varieties such as wasabi leaves or sea aster for a bit of an adventure. I also love adding coriander and amaranth shoots to this salad because they're so fragrant and visual. For more easily accessible ingredients, go for shredded spinach, chard or pak choi.

This recipe is a twist on the classic strawberries and cream, which is such a summer winner. You could even dispense with the mousse altogether and enjoy this scented salad on its own, with shavings of white chocolate and a little orange peel finely zested over the top, in which case it serves 4.

360 calories per portion
2 of your five-a-day

Strawberry Salad with White Chocolate Mousse

Serves 8

200g good white chocolate (with vanilla seeds if possible)

150ml double cream

3 large free-range egg whites

a pinch salt

50g caster sugar

For the strawberry salad

1kg fresh strawberries, washed, hulled and diced

3 tbsp Grand Marnier

2 tbsp freshly squeezed orange juice

40g caster sugar

Break the chocolate into small chunks and melt in a bowl over a saucepan of boiling water with the cream.

Whilst the chocolate is melting, beat the egg whites with the salt until soft peak stage. Next, add the sugar gradually and continue to beat the egg whites until stiff.

Scoop a generous spoonful of the egg white into the melted chocolate and beat together with a rubber spatula.

Next fold half of the remaining egg white carefully into the white chocolate mixture until the air pockets have disappeared. Repeat this process with the remaining egg white, handling the mixture with caution so as not to knock out too much air.

Spoon the mousse into the bottoms of eight tumblers or wine glasses – the mousse should come a third of the way up the glasses. Refrigerate for 2 hours whilst you put together the strawberry salad.

To make the salad, simply mix all the ingredients together in a bowl and allow to stand in the ambient kitchen temperature whilst the mousses chill and set.

Top the mousse with the strawberry salad and serve.

Swap in ... If you don't want to use alcohol in the salad, replace the Grand Marnier with more freshly squeezed orange juice.

There are a handful of recipes in this book that mark the holidays for me – this is one of them. If I'm not yet on holiday, this salad makes me *feel* like I am because it includes so many sunshine ingredients. And when the sun is shining, there is nowhere I prefer to spend the summer than right here in Britain, where you wait all year to snap runner beans right from the plant.

435 calories per portion
2 of your five-a-day

Summer Holiday Runner Bean Salad

Serves 2

280g runner beans, topped, tailed and string removed

2 tbsp olive oil + 1 tbsp for the dressing

1 small seeded bun, torn into crouton-sized chunks

2 tbsp capers

zest and freshly squeezed juice of 1 unwaxed lemon

2 tbsp lemon thyme leaves

2 cloves garlic, minced to a paste

salt and pepper, to taste

a handful baby chard leaves, washed and drained

30g Parmesan, shaved

Put a kettle of water on to boil.

Cut the beans on the diagonal into chunks. Blanch them in boiling water for 2 minutes only. They will be bright green and still quite crunchy. Drain and cool under the cold water tap. Set aside.

Heat 2 tbsp olive oil in a medium frying pan and fry the bread until golden and crispy. Set aside.

Heat the remaining 1 tbsp oil in the same pan with the capers, lemon zest and lemon thyme and cook until it smells fragrant.

Next add the garlic and the cooked beans for a further minute. Season with salt and pepper, then turn off the heat.

Combine the flavoured beans with the croutons and the chard leaves. Toss to combine. Squeeze a little lemon juice over and sprinkle with Parmesan before serving.

Swap in ... Toasted and roughly chopped hazelnuts instead of the croutons if you prefer to go gluten-free. Anchovies, capers and sunblush tomatoes give this salad a Sicilian kick and beef it up a notch if you're really hungry. I also like to replace the Parmesan with semi-hard goat's cheese and matchsticks of raw beetroot, for a change.

This salad is a deconstructed version of the winter stew, made up with raw vegetables. Because all the ingredients in a traditional ratatouille are at their ripe best in summer, this makes for a delicious, fresh and full-flavoured alternative to the classic version. The salad is improved by being made a little ahead and is also sensational with a barbecue.

206 calories per portion
5 of your five-a-day

Summer Ratatouille
with anchovies and lemon

Serves 4

1 large aubergine, cut into small dice

2 medium courgettes, topped, tailed and cut into very small dice

4 tbsp olive oil

1 large Spanish onion, peeled and cut into fine dice

1 medium yellow pepper, cored and chopped into small cubes

1 medium orange pepper, cored and chopped into small cubes

2 cloves garlic, crushed to a paste

3 anchovies, very finely chopped

plenty of salt and pepper

10 medium, ripe tomatoes on the vine

freshly squeezed juice of ½ lemon

a handful basil leaves, torn from the stem

Heat a large frying pan until very hot.

Toss the aubergine and courgette cubes in the olive oil until evenly coated. Add them to the hot frying pan and cook over a high heat for 5 minutes, until the edges have turned a golden colour. You may find that you need to do this stage in two batches.

Tip the hot vegetables into a large bowl with the diced onion, prepared peppers, garlic and anchovies. Season generously with salt and pepper, then cover with cling film. Set aside for 10 minutes, whilst you prepare the tomatoes.

Chop the tomatoes in half and scoop out the seeds and centre with the help of a spoon. Finely chop the flesh, then add to the bowl with the rest of the ingredients.

Finally, squeeze the lemon juice over the salad. Set aside (wrapped in cling film) for an hour in the ambient temperature of your kitchen to let the flavours mingle and develop.

Scatter the basil leaves over just before serving and adjust the seasoning one last time. Serve with crusty bread.

Swap in ... You don't have to add the anchovies by any means, though I like the savouriness that they bring – but this ratatouille is delicious without them. You could include pine nuts if you want the salad to be a little more hearty. Feta or Mozzarella chunks are lovely thrown in at the last minute.

Warming and simple, this hearty salad is a good end to a wet summer's day when you get home and want to knock up dinner in about 10 minutes flat. If you don't have cannellini beans, you could use borlotti, black-eyed beans or even kidney beans. If you don't want to make the pesto from scratch, make sure you buy a fresh, loose-textured, bright-green version.

746 calories per portion
3½ of your five-a-day

Summer Store-cupboard Salad
of cannellini beans, artichoke hearts and salami

Serves 4

1 x 390g tin artichoke hearts, drained

2 x 390g tins cannellini beans, drained and rinsed

4 tbsp Lime and Coriander Pesto (see page 190)

2 tbsp olive oil

100g Milano salami, roughly torn

200g sunblush tomatoes (also called 'semi-dried'), drained of oil and roughly chopped

100g pitted black olives

a small handful coriander leaves

Slice the artichokes into halves or quarters, depending on the size. Toss the beans with the pesto and olive oil. Next, add the salami, tomatoes and olives.

Finally, add the artichoke hearts and scatter a few coriander leaves over before serving.

This salad is also really lovely warm. Simply heat the beans with the olive oil in a small saucepan until hot. Transfer to a bowl and continue with the recipe as before.

Swap in... I made a vegetarian version with Mozzarella and no salami, which was a real winner.

Simple. Delicious. Bright orange, *vibrant* salad . . . This is my kind of food. On its own or on the side of lamb chops with a yoghurt and mint dip, this is what I eat when I want to take care of myself and have fun with it. I don't always buy organic fruit and vegetables – frankly, it's just too expensive – but you can *really* taste the difference here. Organic carrots are much sweeter and fresher than the other ones.

297 calories per portion
2½ of your five-a-day

Warm Salad of Roasted Carrots
with feta, pine nuts and a sweet chilli and tomato glaze

Serves 2

5 medium organic carrots, peeled and cut in quarters lengthways

2 tsp olive oil

2 tbsp Sweet Chilli and Tomato Glaze (page 187), or shop-bought sweet chilli sauce

plenty of salt

40g feta, crumbled

30g pine nuts, toasted in a dry frying pan until golden

2 wedges lime (optional)

Preheat the oven to 200°C/400°F/gas mark 6. Line a flat baking sheet with baking paper.

Toss the carrots in the olive oil. Place in the middle of the hot oven for 25 minutes, after which they will be coloured around the edges and still be lovely and crunchy inside.

Drizzle the Sweet Chilli and Tomato Glaze over the top. Cool for 5 minutes, then season generously with salt.

Assemble the salad by scattering the feta and pine nuts over. Serve with a wedge of lime. Voilà!

Swap in ... I sometimes like to replace the pine nuts with toasted pumpkin seeds, a little Gorgonzola and a handful of oak leaf lettuce in this salad. It's surprising how well Gorgonzola and Sweet Chilli and Tomato Glaze go together. And if it's meat that you're after, add some chopped slices of chorizo and throw over a scattering of coriander.

This salad is where this book began, since it was whilst knocking up a version of this for a dinner party in Paris a year ago that the idea for a salad book came to me . . . As usual, I put it to my chums who were there at the time. For their resounding enthusiasm and 'Go for it!', I want to dedicate this recipe to Jo, Romilly and Camilla G.

295 calories per portion
4½ of your five-a-day

Watermelon, Feta, Spinach and Mint

Serves 4

1kg watermelon, peeled, cubed and de-seeded

200g baby spinach, washed and dried

300g cucumber, peeled and cubed

a small bunch fresh mint leaves (the smaller the leaves, the softer)

250g feta, broken into chunks

4 tbsp Balsamic Glaze (shop-bought, or see page 186)

Combine all the ingredients in a large bowl. Drizzle the Balsamic Glaze over and give the salad a toss before serving.

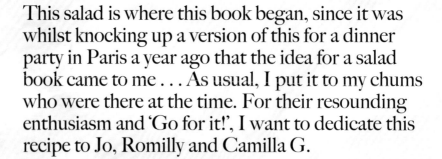

Swap in ... This salad is delicious as it is, just minus the spinach if you want a more refreshing, cool finish. I've also enjoyed adding toasted pumpkin seeds for a little extra texture. You can add basil as well as mint. I sometimes also use plain balsamic vinegar, as opposed to the glaze, and that works well too.

Autumn

This warm salad is a bit of a wacky combination: half French, half Vietnamese and with some other unexpected flavours thrown in. If you've never had a deep-fried egg, you're in for such a surprise! Chanterelles impart so much flavour, but if you want to make this salad when wild mushrooms are out of season, try a mixture of chestnut mushrooms, sliced portobello, shiitake, enoki and even button.

237 calories per portion
2 of your five-a-day

A Salad of Mushrooms and Deep-fried Egg

Serves 4

600g mixed mushrooms, wiped clean with kitchen paper and cut into halves or quarters

1 tbsp olive oil

10g butter

salt and white pepper

4 spring onions, finely chopped

1 tbsp truffle oil

1 tsp Balsamic Glaze (shop-bought, or see page 186)

a head round lettuce, broken into big leaves, washed and spun dry

a small handful parsley, finely chopped

For the deep-fried egg

500ml vegetable oil

4 medium, very fresh free-range eggs

Heat a large frying pan with the olive oil until hot. Add the mushrooms to the pan. Cook until they are golden-brown, then add the butter and cook for another 2 minutes, until the butter has been totally absorbed.

Once the mushrooms are cooked, turn off the heat, season generously with salt and white pepper and scatter the chopped spring onions over. Drizzle with the truffle oil, then the Balsamic Glaze. Toss to combine.

Heat the vegetable oil in a small saucepan – when it is hot it will start to shimmer in the pan. Carefully drop in a little bit of bread to gauge the temperature. You want the bread to react to the oil within a few seconds – then you know the temperature is right.

Next, crack an egg (this is a one-by-one job) into a small bowl and lower it over the hot oil. Carefully drop the egg into the middle of the oil then stand back. Count to 45 in your head, then remove the egg from the oil with a slotted spoon and place it on a plate covered in kitchen paper. Repeat the process until all the eggs are done.

Finally, layer up big leaves of lettuce with mushrooms and spring onions, top with the deep-fried egg and sprinkle with parsley. Serve warm with crusty bread.

Swap in ... Replace truffle oil with strips of cured ham, such as Serrano or Parma, as well as some freshly snipped chives. This salad is also lovely with a poached egg.

440 calories per portion
2½ of your five-a-day

Serves 6

freshly squeezed juice of
½ lemon

1 medium avocado,
cut into squares

salt and pepper, to taste

3 large free-range eggs,
boiled for 7 minutes

This salad allegedly originated in California in the 1930s, at the Hollywood Brown Derby restaurant, where it became their signature dish. Cobb salads vary from place to place and it's not unusual to find ingredients that range from mango and seafood in the southern states, to chicken and blue cheese in the north-east. This hearty salad is traditionally served with the leaves underneath and all the fun stuff on top, divided into sections.

Classic Cobb Salad

200g streaky smoked bacon

2 onions, finely sliced

2 tbsp plain flour

3 tbsp vegetable oil

8 medium, ripe tomatoes
on the vine

6 handfuls romaine lettuce,
washed and roughly torn

6 handfuls watercress
leaves, torn from the stem

200g roasted chicken
meat, roughly torn

100g mature Cheddar
cheese, shaved with a
potato-peeler

For the dressing

4 tbsp red wine vinegar

2 tsp Worcestershire sauce

2 tsp freshly squeezed
lemon juice

2 tsp Dijon mustard

2 small garlic cloves,
minced

4 tbsp walnut oil

a good pinch salt

Combine all the dressing ingredients in a clean jam jar and give a good shake. Taste and season if needed.

Squeeze the ½ lemon over the avocado chunks and toss to coat. Season well with salt and pepper. Peel the eggs and roughly chop them.

Fry the bacon in a large, dry frying pan. Once cooked, remove with a slotted spoon and drain on kitchen paper. Lightly wipe the pan with paper but don't wash it.

Next, toss the onion slices in the flour. Heat the vegetable oil in the pan and fry the onion slices over a high heat until golden and crisp all over. Set aside.

Cut the tomatoes across the waist and scoop out the seeds and middle with a teaspoon. Roughly chop the flesh and discard the seeds.

Toss the leaves in half the salad dressing and arrange at the bottom of your serving platter. Next, add the seasoned avocado, followed by the tomatoes, chicken, bacon, chopped eggs, fried onions and cheese. Drizzle the remaining vinaigrette over and serve. When helping yourself, make sure you dig in and get a bit of everything.

Swap in ··· Replace the chicken with turkey or toasted pecans, the Cheddar with blue cheese. Instead of fried onions use spring onions or chopped raw red onions. If you want to go down the seafood road, I suggest using either shrimp or lobster with mango, sweetcorn, chopped jalapeños, fresh lime juice and chopped coriander.

Well, I have two friends coming over for Sunday lunch in an hour and I haven't even laid the table, let alone started cooking either of the two courses . . . This ribbon salad is exactly the kind of recipe that is festive, light yet satisfying and, most importantly here: ready in 30 minutes.

450 calories per portion
2 of your five-a-day

Courgette Ribbons, Pappardelle and Pancetta

Serves 6

300g pancetta cubes

1kg courgette, washed, topped and tailed with skin still on

2 tbsp olive oil

finely grated zest of 2 unwaxed lemons

½ nutmeg, scratched

plenty of salt and black pepper

250g pappardelle

150g ricotta

Fry the pancetta cubes in a dry frying pan until crispy. Remove with a slotted spoon and drain on kitchen paper. Set aside until needed.

Using a potato-peeler, peel the courgettes into ribbons from top to bottom and lay them on a big serving platter with 1 tbsp of the olive oil, the lemon zest, nutmeg and a generous crunch of salt. Toss to mix, then set aside.

Just before serving, cook the pasta according to the packet instructions, then drain off the cooking water. Dump the pasta over the courgette ribbons and add the remaining 1 tbsp olive oil.

Using kitchen tongs, toss together the courgette and pasta until well mixed.

Finally, scatter the crumbled ricotta and the pancetta cubes over the top. Serve warm.

Swap in ...If you want to make this into a vegetarian dish, simply replace the pancetta with a combination of chopped hazelnuts and sun-dried tomatoes.

As a rule, I don't like so called pasta salads. In writing this book, however, I have found that a well-balanced salad with pasta is actually a really wonderful thing. You may be surprised by the quantity of coriander in this recipe. Don't worry! The leaves will mix in with the rest of the ingredients and make up a wonderful, fresh and fragrant green backdrop for everything else. After all, this is a 'salad' rather than a pasta dish with a few green bits . . .

365 calories per portion
1 of your five-a-day

Crab, Chilli and Coriander Seashell Pasta Salad

Serves 4

200g small seashell pasta (conchiglie rigate)

200g sunblush tomatoes (also called 'semi-dried')

2 cloves garlic, finely minced

3 fresh chillies, very finely cubed

salt, to taste

90g coriander leaves, torn from the stem

2 tbsp olive oil, plus a little extra for drizzling

300g fresh white crab meat

Cook the pasta shells according to the packet instructions, then drain.

If the tomatoes are bigger than the size of a small cherry tomato, cut them in half. Otherwise, simply drain off the excess oil and add to the hot pasta shells, along with the garlic, olive oil, crab and chilli. Season to taste.

Finally, add the coriander right before serving, toss thoroughly and drizzle over a little extra olive oil.

Swap in ... I actually made this without any crab and no substitution and it was pure, delicious, simple food. I then tested it with miniature Mozzarella (bocconcini), which was really good too. Toasted pine nuts make a lovely addition in this salad as well.

This recipe is borrowed from my sister, who made it up for a dinner party I was at recently. I like it on its own when I'm in need of a hit of fresh, green food or with a bowl of plain sticky rice on the side. It also goes wonderfully with Thai fishcakes, or on the side of barbecued pork (simply coated in soy sauce and honey). I like this salad nice and spicy, but it's entirely up to you how much chilli you use.

127 calories per portion
1½ of your five-a-day

Cucumber, Chilli and Lime
with crushed peanuts

Serves 4

35g peanuts, roughly chopped

1 large whole cucumber, peeled

½ whole red chilli, cut into fine shreds

a small bunch coriander, roughly chopped

For the peanut dressing

1 tbsp smooth peanut butter

freshly squeezed juice of 1 lime

1 small clove garlic, grated finely

1 tsp clear honey

1 tsp nam plah (Thai fish sauce)

Toast the chopped peanuts in a dry frying pan for 5 minutes over a medium-high heat until golden. Remove from the pan and set aside.

To make the dressing, loosen the peanut butter with the lime juice, whisking with a fork until smooth, then add the grated garlic, honey and nam plah. This recipe is particularly great if you want to use up the bottom of a peanut butter jar, etc. Shake well to combine.

Cut the cucumber down the centre lengthways. Using a teaspoon, scrape out the seeds. Next, slice the cucumber into thin half moons.

Toss the cucumber in the dressing to coat. Add the chilli and chopped peanuts and toss again. Finally, scatter the coriander over and serve.

Swap in ... Add in some grilled shrimp, rice vermicelli and a little sesame oil for a more substantial meal. Plus, when I can lay my hands on some (it's a bit difficult to locate most of the time), I like to add thinly sliced green papaya to the glass noodle and shrimp version of this salad.

This is another one of my 'hybrid' salads, which is to say that I made up a recipe that doesn't really belong to any particular cuisine, although I suspect it would come from somewhere hot and aromatic, like Iran or Lebanon, with a dash of America thrown into the mix in the form of a light, fennel coleslaw. At any rate, it's absolutely delicious and is a vibrant, colourful autumn favourite of mine.

557 calories per portion
2½ of your five-a-day

Fennel and Mint with halloumi and harissa

Serves 4

4 small fennel bulbs or two large ones, halved then shaved super-fine (if I don't have a mandoline to shave the fennel thinly, I use a very sharp knife – the thinness of the fennel is key to the texture and taste of this recipe)

2 unwaxed lemons

180g thick, plain yoghurt

4 small cloves garlic, grated on a fine grater

2 tbsp tahini paste

salt, to taste

3 tbsp rose harissa (I like to use Belazu)

300g Halloumi cheese, cut into ½cm strips

60g plain flour

2 tsp olive oil

a large handful mint, finely shredded

seeds of 1 large pomegranate

Toss the shaved fennel in a large mixing bowl with the juice from one of the lemons to prevent it browning. Next, mix up the yoghurt, minced garlic and tahini paste until well combined. Taste and season with salt until you're happy. Dress the fennel with the yoghurt mixture and divide between four plates.

Next, spoon out the harissa on to a large plate and add the Halloumi. Coat the cheese pieces with the help of a fork or using kitchen gloves, as this stuff stains! Tip the flour on to another large plate, add the harissa-coated cheese slices and toss to coat them in flour.

Heat a frying pan until very hot. Add some of the olive oil and tilt the pan to spread evenly. Next, add the cheese and fry for 2 minutes on each side, until crispy. If your pan isn't big enough, cook them in batches, adding a little more oil as necessary. Once the cheese is cooked, divide between the four plates.

Finally, top with plenty of mint and the pomegranate seeds. Squeeze the juice from the other lemon over everything and serve straight away.

Swap in ··· Toasted almond flakes and slices of grilled lamb instead of the Halloumi. Replace the harissa paste with fresh, chopped chilli, added to the salad at the end. Add in sliced red onions, shredded iceberg lettuce and stuff into a warm pitta pocket for a different take on a kebab.

I spent the first four years of my life living in the Middle East. Although most of my memories are a blur of incadescent white heat and sand, I remember two things vividly: the banana tree in the garden and *kebbeh* – the miniature rugby balls made of ground lamb, semolina and spices. This recipe is a mish-mash between a traditional Lebanese couscous and parsley salad (*tabbouleh*) and the aromatic flavour of the *kebbeh*.

460 calories per portion
4 of your five-a-day

Autumn Store-cupboard Salad
of kebbeh tabbouleh

Serves 6

250g quinoa or bulgur wheat (or a mixture of both)

1 vegetable stock cube

4 tbsp olive oil

1.2kg aubergine (or 5 small ones), topped, tailed and cut into 2cm cubes

1kg large tomatoes, washed under the tap

a good pinch salt

60g flat-leaf parsley, roughly chopped

2 medium red onions, cut into small dice

120g pine nuts

1 heaped tsp mixed spice

Cook the quinoa or bulgur wheat according to the packet instructions, remembering to add the stock cube to the pan with the water. Once cooked, drain.

Heat half the olive oil in a large frying pan. When it's hot, add half the aubergine cubes and cook until golden on all sides (roughly 8 minutes). Once cooked, remove and set aside before repeating with the other half of the oil and aubergine. Aubergine sweats a great deal, which is why it's important to cook it in two batches and give it a chance to colour. Also, it's a good idea to avoid adding salt at this stage or you will end up with steamed aubergine, rather than fried. Set aside when all the aubergine is cooked.

Next, cut the tomatoes across the waist and scoop out the watery bit in the middle with a spoon. Roughly chop the hollowed-out tomatoes into medium dice.

Mix together the cooked quinoa, tomatoes and aubergine with a generous pinch of salt and the remaining ingredients. Toss to combine and serve at room temperature.

Swap in ... You can use couscous instead of bulgur wheat or quinoa, using exactly the same method. For slightly more pronounced flavour, use a lamb stock cube instead of vegetable. Add grated lemon zest, sumac and pomegranate seeds for a citrus twist on this recipe.

This fruit salad was passed on to me via my beloved Aunty Sarah, who got it from Mrs D, whose daughter Lizzie was in the same class as Sophie, my cousin, in Richmond, some twenty years ago, which is when Sarah tried it for the first time . . . You get the picture. This recipe has been loved and handed around because it's just that *blinking* good. It used to have butter in it but I didn't think it improved it, so I took it out.

288 calories per portion
2 of your five-a-day

Mrs Davidson's Autumn Fruit Salad

Serves 4

2 figs, washed and cut into halves

4 plums, cut in halves and stoned

4 yellow-fleshed nectarines, cut into halves and stoned

80g soft brown sugar

200ml Marsala

30g toasted almonds

Preheat the oven to 180°C/350°F/gas mark 4.

Place the fruit and sugar in an ovenproof dish at the bottom of the hot oven. Add the Marsala and cook for 45 minutes. The fruit should be softened but still retain its shape.

Cool for 20 minutes, basting with the syrup. Scatter over the toasted almonds before serving.

This recipe is lovely with a side of crème fraîche, mixed with the seeds from a vanilla pod as well as 1 tsp honey. I also like it with a dry biscuit, like a *cantuccini*.

Swap in . . . Peaches, pears, slices of pineapple, apricots if still available (you can even used tinned ones for this).

This is a variety of coleslaw that I came across in Chicago recently that had no mayonnaise. I don't like coleslaw when it's either dripping with cream or stiff with mayonnaise – or a miserable combination of the two. At its core, coleslaw is a lightly pickled cabbage salad, flavoured with spices and a variety of other thinly grated vegetables. I like this light slaw on hot dogs, beef or cheese sandwiches. It's also lovely with any kind of barbecue.

254 calories per portion
3 of your five-a-day

Old-fashioned Slaw

Serves 4

400g white cabbage, tough
   outer leaves removed

250g celeriac, peeled and
   tailed

1 onion

200g carrot, peeled

3 tbsp cider vinegar

1 tsp poppy seeds

1 tbsp caster sugar

a good crunch white pepper

1½ tsp salt

4 tbsp vegetable oil

1 tbsp mayonnaise (I like
   Hellmann's)

3 spring onions, finely
   sliced

Using a mandoline or a very sharp knife, finely shred the cabbage, celeriac, onion and carrots.

Place in a large bowl with the vinegar, poppy seeds, sugar, white pepper and salt. Toss to combine, then add the oil and the mayonnaise and mix well. Allow to stand for 30 minutes before serving so that the flavours can develop.

Scatter the chopped spring onions over and serve at room temperature. Keeps in the fridge for 2 days.

Swap in ... Sliced apple or pear, gherkins, mustard seeds, sunflower seeds, red cabbage (this will give you a pink coleslaw!), raisins.

Sometimes you need a hit of warmth and colour to help with the cool grey days of autumn. The ingredients in this salad are Spanish, but I'm taking liberties since I have never had it in Spain, nor even heard of such a dish. This salad is actually straight from travels in my mind and fantasies of colourful, aromatic food at a time of year when the days grow ever more glum and damp.

312 calories per portion
3 of your five-a-day

Orange and Yellow Spanish Salad

Serves 6

2 large onions, cut into very small dice

2 tbsp olive oil

a generous pinch saffron

2 x 400g tins butter beans, drained and rinsed under the tap

180g red pepper, sliced into long strips and de-seeded

200g yellow and orange peppers, de-seeded and cut into long strips

2 tbsp sherry vinegar

¾ tsp salt

100g rocket leaves, washed and spun

100g chorizo slices, cut into strips

100g roasted almonds, roughly chopped

Fry the diced onion in the olive oil in a very large frying pan with the saffron and drained beans. Cook with the lid on for 15 minutes over a low heat, then add the pepper slices. Cover again and cook for a final 15 minutes on a medium heat.

Turn off the heat, then add the sherry vinegar. Season to taste.

Add three quarters of the rocket to the warm contents of the pan and toss briefly.

Divide the warm salad between the plates, before scattering with the chorizo, almonds and remaining rocket.

Swap in ...I had this salad again the next day as a veggie version without the chorizo. I added a fried egg and a pinch of paprika on top of the warmed salad: totally delicious.

There isn't a banana season in the UK that I'm aware of, so this is seasonal to me because it's the kind of warming, rich and utterly indulgent dessert that I can't get enough of when the weather turns cold. You can replace the rum in the butterscotch with water if you prefer – personally, I adore the combination of rum and bananas. My father does a mean *Banane Flambée au rum*, but that's another story!

255 calories per portion
½ of your five-a-day

Pan-fried Bananas with Rum Butterscotch

Serves 4

2 large bananas, or 4 baby ones

50g unsalted butter

100g golden syrup

3 tbsp dark rum

a pinch salt

1 tbsp sesame seeds, toasted in a dry frying pan until golden

Cut the bananas in half lengthways, still in their skins.

Heat up a dry non-stick frying pan until hot. Place the bananas cut side down on to the hot surface of the pan and cook them for 2 minutes. Then turn them skin side down and give them another few minutes. You can also do this step under the grill. Set aside.

To make the rum butterscotch, melt the butter, golden syrup and rum in a medium saucepan over a low heat until everything in the pan is liquid. Next, turn up the heat and, once you reach boiling point, set your kitchen timer for 3 minutes *exactly* of hard boiling. It's tempting to fiddle with the mixture in the pan, but I urge you just to let it do its own thing undisturbed.

When the 3 minutes are up, take the pan off the heat immediately and start beating the mixture with a balloon whisk until all the bubbles have disappeared. Add the pinch of salt at this point and stir to dissolve.

Drizzle the butterscotch over the warm bananas and sprinkle with toasted sesame seeds. Serve immediately, before the butterscotch starts to set. This is devilish with vanilla, ginger or *dulce de leche* ice cream.

Swap in ... You could replace the toasted sesame seeds with toasted unsalted peanuts or cashews. And rum butterscotch goes with *everything*, in my opinion! Try it over ice cream, baked pineapple, drizzled over chocolate cake. The list is endless . . .

This recipe is on loan from my friend Olivia, whose boss hails from Baghdad. I was handed a rough ingredients list, and excitedly got testing. This is a truly uplifting sight on your plate and is very refreshing. I like it by itself, with a little warm, fresh pitta bread. It also works beautifully with lamb or chicken kebabs for the last of the year's barbecues.

155 calories per portion
3½ of your five-a-day

Persian Salad of Tomato, Pomegranate and Cucumber

Serves 2

300g ripe cherry tomatoes on the vine, cut in quarters

½ medium cucumber, peeled and cut lengthways

seeds from 1 medium pomegranate

a small bunch parsley, leaves only

a small bunch coriander, leaves only

a small bunch mint, very finely chopped

3 spring onions, very finely sliced

1 tsp sumac

For the dressing

1 tbsp olive oil

2 tsp freshly squeezed lemon juice

plenty of salt and pepper

Rinse the tomatoes thoroughly under the tap and let them stand in a colander to drip off the excess water. This is a nifty way to loosen most of the seeds and wash them away.

Next, core the cucumber by running a teaspoon down the middle and removing all the seeds. Chop into smallish dice of roughly the same size.

In a medium bowl, combine the drained tomatoes, pomegranate seeds, cucumber, parsley, coriander, mint, spring onion and sumac. Mix the dressing ingredients together and season generously.

Toss the salad in the dressing and serve right away.

Swap in ... This salad is great with a handful of baby spinach or other young leaf varieties. Add toasted pine nuts or flaked almonds for a bit of extra crunch and sustenance. Some crumbled feta is delicious here, as well as a little fresh red chilli.

I'm not crazy about roasted vegetables. I can hear you all crying out that they're wonderful, but something about them slightly *bores* me. That said, the colours you can end up with on your plate are wonderful. This recipe is particularly bright and because of the magic of the Sweet Chilli and Tomato Glaze, it has a little unexpected bite that peps up the whole salad. If you haven't tried it this way before, get cracking and make it now – if not sooner!

395 calories per portion
2½ of your five-a-day

Roasted Root Vegetables with Crispy Garlic Pitta

Serves 4

1 red onion, peeled and cut into 6 wedges

1 yellow pepper, de-seeded and quartered

1 red pepper, de-seeded and quartered

1 courgette, cut into diagonal slices

160g butternut squash, peeled and cut into 1cm-thick half moons

2 tbsp olive oil + a little more for brushing over the pitta

1 pitta bread

plenty of salt

1 small clove garlic

250g buffalo Mozzarella, torn into chunks

4 tbsp Sweet Chilli and Tomato Glaze (page 187)

a small handful torn basil

Preheat the oven to 200°C/400°F/gas mark 6. Line a baking sheet with tinfoil. Toss the prepared root vegetables with the olive oil and put on the baking sheet. Cook in the middle of the hot oven for 30 minutes in total.

Cut the pitta open with the tip of a knife so that you end up with two flat oval halves. Brush each rough side with the extra olive oil. When the vegetables have had 20 minutes in the oven, put the pitta in the oven next to the vegetables. You can place it straight on to the wire rack as this will crisp it up even more.

When the vegetables and the pitta are done, remove from the oven and sprinkle with a pinch of salt. Rub the rough side of the pitta halves with the garlic (as much or as little as you like).

Arrange the vegetables on a large serving dish with the Mozzarella and pour the Sweet Chilli and Tomato Glaze over the top. Break the crispy pitta on top. Finally, scatter with the basil. Serve warm.

Swap in ... A little roast chicken for the Mozzarella. You can also use olives and a little salami or some fried pancetta instead of Mozzarella. Add a handful of fresh baby spinach over the top for an extra hit of green. It is also absolutely divine with cubes of blue cheese and toasted walnuts instead of the Mozzarella and pitta.

What a glum and gloomy grey Tuesday afternoon in late September. I have a sudden craving for warm, orange, melting *something*... I'm desperately clinging on to summer and the green leaves on the leaves, but on a day like today it's all about autumn and comfort. Although I plan to eat this salad for supper tonight curled up in front of *Spooks*, this recipe is a wonderful candidate for dinner parties too.

335 calories per portion
3 of your five-a-day

Roasted Squash with Thyme and Taleggio

Serves 4

600g mixed squashes (such as acorn, butternut, pumpkin), seeds removed

2 tbsp olive oil

salt and pepper, to taste

2 large red onions, cut into thin moons

2 tbsp thyme leaves, stripped from the stalk

200g Taleggio cheese, cut into cubes

2 generous handfuls rocket leaves, washed and dried

For the dressing

3 tbsp balsamic vinegar

1 tbsp maple syrup

plenty of salt

Preheat the oven to 200 ° C/400 ° F/gas mark 6.

Cut the squashes into half moons of around 2cm thickness. Toss them in the olive oil and roast in the top of the oven for 5 minutes. Make sure to spread the squash on to a large baking sheet so that they roast, as opposed to steam. Leave the seasoning with salt until right at the end for the same reason.

Turn the oven setting to grill. Remove the tray from the oven and add the red onion slices to the cooked squash, sprinkle with the thyme and place back in the oven. Grill for a further 10 minutes or until the squash looks blistered and golden.

Meanwhile, make the dressing. Mix the balsamic vinegar and maple syrup with a pinch of salt in a small saucepan. Bring to the boil and boil hard for 5 minutes. The syrup will now be thickened and glossy.

When the squash and onions have had their time, remove from the oven and pile on to a large serving platter. Taste and season with salt and pepper. Dot the Taleggio cubes all over and give it a good toss. Scatter the rocket over the top. Drizzle with the warm glaze and give a final mix, taking care not to break up the squash. Serve warm.

Swap in ... This is great with Fontina instead of Taleggio and sage instead of thyme. Add croutons for extra crunch and an autumn leaf like oak leaf instead of rocket for a bigger-all-round salad.

403 calories per portion
½ of your five-a-day

This is a salad that was inspired by my time working as a waitress at La Boissonerie in rue de Seine. It's a wonderful peppy, easy salad to have as a side to grilled fish, pan-fried chicken or lamb chops. It works wonders as a starter too.

Rocket, Dates and Hazelnut Pesto

Serves 4

4 generous handfuls rocket, washed and dried

8 tablespoons Hazelnut Pesto (page 191), loosened with 1 tbsp lemon juice

6 plump dates, pitted and roughly chopped

20g Parmesan, shaved thinly

Toss the rocket leaves in a large bowl with half the pesto. This will coat the leaves and mean that the salad is seasoned throughout.

Scatter the chopped dates over the salad. Drizzle with the remaining pesto and scatter the Parmesan shavings before serving.

Swap in ... Balsamic vinegarette (page 188) instead of the pesto. If you do this, I recommend adding some additional toasted hazelnuts or almonds for texture.

There is a version of this salad in most brasseries and little bistros around Paris. The ingredients vary widely, but you will likely always find thin strips of either Gruyère or Emmental cheese and either ham or chicken, as well as boiled new potatoes – all nestled in a giant green salad. It's a real favourite of mine because it's quick, easy to prepare, and satisfying without being too heavy.

340 calories per portion
2 of your five-a-day

Serves 6

300g haricots verts

500g new potatoes, scrubbed

4 large free-range eggs

8 large handfuls either mixed continental leaves or round lettuce, washed and dried

4 thin slices Emmental, cut into thin strips

4 thin slices roast ham, cut into thin strips

6 medium-sized, ripe tomatoes, cut into six

60g pitted black olives

a handful chives, finely chopped

For the dressing

a small handful parsley

1 shallot, finely diced

2 tbsp Dijon mustard

2 tbsp white wine vinegar (or Honey and Tarragon vinegar see page 192)

2 tsp runny honey

3 tbsp olive oil

salt and white pepper

Salade Parisienne

Bring a saucepan of hot water to the boil. Blanch the beans in boiling water for 1 minute then remove with a slotted spoon and run cold water over them before setting aside.

Boil the potatoes until tender in the same pan as the beans were cooked. Add the eggs to the water 5 minutes before the end of their cooking time.

Drain, then run cold water over the potatoes and eggs until they feel cool to the touch.

Chop the potatoes into roughly similar-sized pieces, peel the eggs and cut them in half.

Put all the ingredients for the salad dressing in a clean jam jar and give a good shake. Toss the salad leaves and chopped potatoes in the dressing before adding the remaining ingredients. Scatter with the chives and serve.

Swap in ... This salad is pretty much an open-ended recipe, but the ingredients above are the most traditional in a Salade Parisienne. Replace Emmental with Gruyère, ham with roast chicken. It's lovely as a take on a Niçoise, with tuna and basil instead of the meat and cheese. Or replace the potatoes with croutons and swap in sweetcorn for haricot beans.

595 calories per portion
5 of your five-a-day

Serves 6

For the root beer brisket

1.5kg brisket of beef

1 tbsp vegetable oil

5 cloves garlic, smashed
then roughly chopped

100g shallots, peeled and
roughly chopped

5 allspice seeds, or 1 tsp
ground allspice

1 tsp salt

60g soft brown sugar

1 tbsp tomato ketchup

350ml root beer

¼ tsp cayenne pepper (less
if you don't like it hot)

1 x 300ml pot sour cream
and chopped chives
(optional)

For the salad

2 x 400g tins black beans

corn from 4 cobs, boiled
until cooked

4 cloves garlic, smashed
then minced into a paste

freshly squeezed juice
from 2 large limes

2 tbsp red wine vinegar

2 tbsp vegetable oil

400g ripe cherry tomatoes,
roughly chopped

1 green jalapeño chilli,
de-seeded, de-veined
and finely diced

a large handful coriander,
roughly chopped

4 shallots, very finely diced

salt, to taste

2 heads iceberg lettuce,
broken into leaves

I was a bridesmaid at a wedding in North Carolina last year. I fell in love with the American South, with its shrimp boats, hair-dos, fried green tomatoes, grits and wrap-around verandas. Any leftover meat from this recipe can go into the most insanely wonderful sandwiches: hot dog bun, warm brisket, mayonnaise, English mustard, gherkins and Old-fashioned Slaw (page 117). Danny thinks I should sell these at festivals!

Southern Salad with Root Beer Brisket

Preheat the oven to 140°C/275°F/gas mark 1.

Fry the beef with the oil in a very large casserole pan until golden all over. Remove and set aside. Add the garlic, shallots, allspice, salt, sugar, ketchup, root beer and cayenne pepper to the pan. Stir to dissolve. Finally, add the browned beef and any juices that may have formed from resting. Put the lid back on the pan and place in the middle of the oven. Cook without peeking for 3 hours, then give the mixture a stir (scraping up any bits at the bottom) and turn the beef over, before replacing it for the remaining 3 hours of cooking. The total cooking time is 6 hours.

To make the salad, drain the beans and rinse under cold water. Make the dressing by combining the garlic, lime juice, vinegar and oil in a large bowl. Next, add all the ingredients except the lettuce and stir. Season with salt and add a little more chilli if you like it hotter.

To make the lettuce wraps, add some shredded warm brisket to the middle of a lettuce leaf and spoon over some salad. Roll up and enjoy!

You can also serve with a small bowl of sour cream and chives if you want something to temper the heat from the chilli.

Swap in … A little *queso fresco* or feta is a delicious replacement for the meat. Avocado also works if you want to go vegetarian. Swap root beer for Coca-Cola and double up the allspice.

The summer is tapering into autumn but I'm not quite ready to let go of sunshine ingredients like figs and almonds. The best cut of lamb for this recipe is fillet but it is so wildly expensive that I've opted for lamb steaks. I often serve this with toasted sourdough that has been rubbed with garlic, a little salt and drizzled with olive oil. I've deliberately chosen lovely full plates here because the ingredients are so fresh and healthy.

438 calories per portion
1 of your five-a-day

Spinach, Lamb and Fig
with orange and honey dressing

Serves 4

60g slivered almonds

2 tsp olive oil

800g lamb steaks, trimmed of any fat

salt and pepper

4 generous handfuls baby spinach, washed and dried

4 ripe figs, cut into quarters

For the dressing

freshly squeezed juice and finely grated zest of 1 orange

2 tsp olive oil

2 tsp runny honey

Toast the almonds in a large dry frying pan for a few minutes until they turn golden, remembering to flip them from time to time. Set aside to cool.

In the same frying pan, turn up the heat until smoking hot and add the olive oil. Fry the lamb leg steaks for roughly a minute on each side (depending on the thickness). You're looking for a rich brown colour on each side. Season generously with salt and pepper and set aside to rest. It's better to do the frying in two batches than to overcrowd the pan, since this will steam the lamb as opposed to searing it.

To make the dressing, combine the ingredients in a large salad bowl and add the spinach leaves. Toss to coat them lightly.

Cut the lamb steaks into horizontal, thin strips so that the pink middle contrasts with the darker edges.

Pile the plates high with the dressed spinach before adding the figs and sliced lamb. Scatter the almonds over and serve straight away.

Swap in … Replacing the lamb with a strong blue cheese such as Gorgonzola or Roquefort is a wonderful vegetarian variation of this recipe.

Almost everyone I ever speak to about tofu crinkles their nose at me when I say that I really like it. I expect that they haven't tried it in a really lovely stir-fry, when it soaks up all the ambient flavours and gives you a lovely texture change within the salad. This is a quick and easy recipe, which is full of flavour; perfect for a week-night supper if you want something light and fragrant.

285 calories per portion
2 of your five-a-day

Stir-fried Tofu, Ginger, Garlic and Broccoli

Serves 2

320g broccoli, broken into florets

1 tbsp sesame oil

150g firm tofu, cut into 1cm cubes

3 cloves garlic, very finely chopped

30g fresh ginger, peeled and very finely chopped

2 tbsp dark soy sauce

1 tbsp clear honey

1 tbsp sesame seeds

Bring a pan of water to the boil. Drop the broccoli florets into the hot water and boil for 2 minutes exactly. Run under cold water then drain in a sieve or colander whilst you finish the rest of the recipe.

Meanwhile, heat the sesame oil in a frying pan. Fry the tofu, garlic and ginger until they smell aromatic and start to sizzle.

Next add the soy sauce and the honey. Allow to reduce for 2 minutes, then pour it over the drained broccoli and toss to coat evenly.

Finally, sprinkle the sesame seeds over and serve warm.

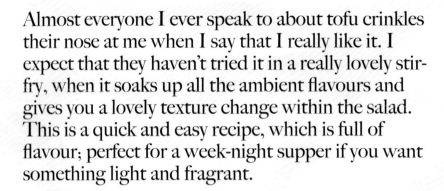

Swap in... A little chopped fresh red chilli, beansprouts, water chestnuts, toasted peanuts instead of sesame seeds. You could also replace the tofu with 200g grilled pork tenderloin medallions or shrimps – cooked in the pan as before.

Thanksgiving takes place on the fourth Thursday in November and is an American holiday that revolves almost entirely around one big, amazing autumnal feast. You'll find most of the traditional Thanksgiving ingredients in this salad, although it's not properly Thanksgiving without pumpkin pie, which is why I have seasoned the squash in this recipe with spices.

445 calories per portion
2 of your five-a-day

Thanksgiving Salad

Serves 2

25g pecan nuts, roughly chopped

25g pumpkin seeds

200g butternut squash, peeled, de-seeded and cut into half moons roughly 1cm thick

2 tsp olive oil

½ tsp mixed spice

2 large handfuls baby spinach

100g thin roast turkey slices, roughly torn

½ red onion, finely sliced

20g dried cranberries

For the dressing

1 tsp runny honey

1 tbsp olive oil

1 tbsp cider vinegar

plenty of salt and pepper

Preheat the oven to 220°C/425°F/gas mark 7.

In a dry frying pan, toast the pecan nuts and pumpkin seeds until golden. Remove from the pan and set aside.

Fry the half moons of squash in the olive oil for a few minutes, until the sides turn golden brown. Sprinkle the mixed spice over and move around the pan to coat evenly. Transfer the squash to a baking sheet and cook in the oven for 10-15 minutes until cooked through.

Whilst the squash is cooking, make the dressing by combining the honey with the olive oil in the warm pan, then whisk in the vinegar and season generously with salt and pepper.

In a large bowl, dress the spinach leaves then add the turkey, toasted nuts and seeds, red onion, cranberries and finally the cooked squash.

Serve whilst the squash is still warm.

Swap in ... I've also cooked this recipe as a vegetarian salad by replacing the turkey with 60g feta, which worked beautifully too.

This salad includes some fairly unusual ingredients but is simple to prepare. It is good for entertaining or for when you want something just a little bit different – the colours are sensational. If you can't find quail, you could use whole partridges, jointed pheasants or guinea fowl.

605 calories per portion
1 of your five-a-day

Warm Salad of Quail, Radicchio, Black Pudding and Walnuts

Serves 4

4 whole quails

15g butter

200g black pudding

24 large red grapes, cut in half (seedless are easiest)

1 head radicchio, washed and cut into thin strips

50g shelled walnuts

2 tsp runny honey

plenty of salt and pepper

2 heads red chicory, cut in half lengthways

a small bunch chives, very finely chopped

For the dressing

4 tsp sherry vinegar

2 tbsp walnut oil

a small pinch cinnamon

2 tsp runny honey

2 tsp Dijon mustard

Preheat the oven to 180°C/350°F/gas mark 4.

Fry the whole quails with the butter over a medium heat until the skin has turned a golden colour. Next, place them in an ovenproof dish and cook for another 10–15 minutes (depending on how cooked you like your bird) in the middle of the hot oven. Remove from the oven and wrap the meat in foil to relax until the rest of the salad is ready.

Fry the black pudding in the same pan as the quails. Just before it's completely cooked, add the grapes and radicchio to warm through. Remove and set aside.

Finally, fire up the heat under the pan and add the walnuts. Toast for a couple of minutes or until golden, then add the honey. Sizzle for a further minute before tipping the contents on to a plate to cool and crunch up. Season generously with salt.

Make up the dressing in a large salad bowl, then add the chicory and warmed radicchio leaves. Season generously with salt and pepper. Give the salad a good toss before dividing between the plates.

Top with the quails, crumble over the black pudding, then add the walnuts, grapes and the chives. Drizzle with any remaining dressing you might have in the bottom of the bowl and serve warm.

Swap in ... If you don't like black pudding, I suggest adding crumbled sausage meat instead. I love the bitterness of radicchio, but if you don't, replace with a softer leaf like red oak lettuce.

Winter

This salad is so full of opulent colours and warming flavours that it actually makes me look forward to winter evenings and long lunches. If you can buy a bunch of beetroot that still has the tops on (the red and green leaves at the top of the stalks), this is a fantastic place to use them. If you can't get hold of any, I suggest replacing them with a couple of handfuls of baby spinach.

350 calories per portion
2 of your five-a-day

Balsamic and Caraway Roasted Beetroot with Goat's Cheese and Hazelnuts

Serves 2

3 tbsp balsamic vinegar

1 tbsp olive oil

3 raw beetroot, washed, tailed and tops reserved

1 tsp caraway seeds

a handful beet tops, or 2 small handfuls baby spinach

1 tbsp clear honey

plenty of salt

20g hazelnuts, toasted in a dry frying pan until golden

a small handful chives

60g goat's cheese log, crumbled (it's better to use a goat's cheese with a slightly chalky middle, like Ragstone, as it's easier to crumble than a squidgy variety)

Preheat the oven to 200°C/400°F/gas mark 6. Line a baking sheet with foil.

Whisk together the balsamic vinegar and olive oil.

Cut each beetroot into six segments and toss with the balsamic mixture. Lay out flat on the prepared baking sheet before sprinkling with the caraway seeds. Roast for 30 minutes in the middle of the hot oven.

Meanwhile, tear the beet tops away from the stalks. Rinse and pat dry.

When the beetroot are cooked, pour the honey on to the hot tray and season generously with salt. Toss to coat evenly.

Mix the tops with the cooked beetroot before dividing between two plates. Finish by scattering with hazelnuts, chives and goat's cheese before serving.

Swap in … You can make this with half beetroot and half pumpkin and scatter with toasted pumpkin seeds. Replace the feta with fried bacon and the honey with maple syrup for a slightly different variation.

Around the Christmas season I need fall-back meals that are good for 'nights off'. I like this light salad when I want a bit of a detox, or if I'm looking for something that's ready in 5 minutes. It's perfect either on its own if you don't want to eat much before going to bed, or on the side of salmon cut into sashimi strips, a pan-seared fillet of fish or a small avocado with lime juice, salt and pepper if you want to eat vegetarian.

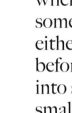

160 calories per portion
1 of your five-a-day

Feel-good Salad

**Serves 1 tired person
in need of some TLC**

a large handful baby
    spinach leaves, washed
    and dried

a small handful coriander,
    roughly chopped

2 spring onions,
    sliced thinly

a little fresh red chilli,
    finely chopped (optional)

1 tbsp sesame seeds

For the dressing

1 tbsp sweet chilli sauce

1 tbsp dark soy sauce

1 tsp sesame oil

Mix the spinach, coriander, spring onions and chilli (if using) on a large plate.

Heat up a dry frying pan until it is very hot and toast the sesame seeds for 30 seconds before tipping them on to a plate. Don't be surprised if they start to jump around! You'll know they're done because they'll look a little tanned.

To make the dressing, combine all the ingredients in a glass and pour into the hot pan. After 10 seconds of warming through, pour it over the salad and sprinkle with the sesame seeds. Enjoy straight away.

Swap in ... This is also a fabulous base salad for adding chopped peanuts, bean shoots, alpha sprouts, deep-fried glass noodles or any manner of other Asian ingredients.

If you fancy having pan-seared salmon with this recipe, I suggest cooking the fish over high heat in the residual cooking juices of the pan for a couple of minutes each side (depending on how cooked you like your fish). This will give it a slightly caramelized edge and it will taste sweet and smoky. Squeeze over a little lime juice, add a dash of soy sauce and off you go.

Although this recipe is in the Winter chapter because this is the time I feel I need the most 'help' from my food to keep my spirits up, this salad is of course suited to all times of the year, since spinach is available all year round.

If you feel anything like me today, you're feeling lazy and 'happy tired'. The fridge is heaving with leftovers (yum, yum) and it is just so great to be able to chuck a salad together, using some of them up and giving yesterday's Christmas dinner a fun, new lease of life that includes some much needed greenery. I often serve this salad warm, on our laps in front of whatever movie we're watching.

600 calories per portion
2 of your five-a-day

Boxing Day Turkey Salad

Serves 6

4 tbsp olive oil

400g leftover bacon rolls, or grilled streaky bacon, broken into bits

600g roast parsnips, potatoes, carrots

2 onions, finely diced

a small handful sage leaves, chopped fine

400g cooked turkey meat, torn into shreds

160g chestnuts or walnuts, roughly chopped

6 large handfuls soft, dark lettuce leaves (such as oak leaf), washed and dried

For the dressing

4 tbsp cranberry jelly (you could also use leftover cranberry sauce)

2 tbsp walnut oil

4 tbsp Raspberry Vinegar (page 192)

Preheat the oven to 200°C/400°F/gas mark 6.

Warm the olive oil in a large roasting tin before adding the bacon rolls, roasted vegetables, chopped onion, sage and turkey meat, along with the chestnuts (if using). If you're using walnuts, toast them in a dry frying pan for 5 minutes until golden, before adding to the rest of the ingredients.

Put in the hot oven for 10 minutes, until all the ingredients are warmed through and infused with the flavours of onion and sage.

Make the dressing by heating up the cranberry jelly in a small saucepan. Once it has become liquid, whisk in the walnut oil and Raspberry Vinegar.

Combine the warm ingredients with the fresh lettuce leaves. Drizzle the dressing over and serve warm.

Swap in ... This recipe is highly adaptable and I suggest that you substitute what you have in your fridge (cooked carrots, sprouts, roast potatoes) for what I have in mine here.

This salad is a reflection of the tastes and textures I am craving at this dark, damp time of the year. Whilst writing this recipe, I confirmed a valuable fact about chillies: the heat of a chilli is ALL in the seeds and veins. First, I only used the flesh of the chillies. Then I added the seeds of one of them . . . Well, the roof of my mouth nearly blew off! Temper the heat of the dressing by adding or removing the seeds.

864 calories per portion
2½ of your five-a-day

Chicken, Avocado and Tortilla Chips with a hot green salsa

Serves 4

1 large or 2 small avocados, peeled and sliced, tossed in freshly squeezed juice of 1 lime

2 medium chicken breasts, with skin on

2 heads romaine lettuce, washed and roughly chopped

1 medium red onion, finely diced

200g plain corn tortilla chips

For the hot green salsa

2 mild green chillies

150ml olive oil

freshly squeezed juice of 2 plump limes

2 tsp runny honey

2 cloves garlic, peeled and smashed with the back of a knife

a large handful coriander leaves, roughly chopped

salt

Place the chillies in a dry frying pan over a high heat until the skin is blistered and black all over. Once the chillies are cool enough to handle, peel off the skin. Remove the seeds and the veins – but see the recipe introduction above if you like your salsa hot. Place the flesh in the bowl of a food processor along with the olive oil, lime juice, honey, garlic, coriander and a good pinch of salt. Pulse until you have a roughly even hot green salsa.

Next, place the chicken breast in a dry frying pan with the skin side down. If you don't have a non-stick frying pan, simply add 1 tsp olive oil to the pan at the beginning of the cooking. Bring gently up to a medium-high heat and flip the breast over when the skin has turned golden, after about 8 minutes. Repeat with the other side. You can check if the meat is done by slicing into the thickest part and having a look.

Once the chicken is cooked, wrap it in foil and set aside whilst you assemble the rest of the salad. Toss the lettuce leaves in half of the hot green salsa. Next add the red onion, avocado slices and tortilla chips. Slice the chicken into medium strips and add to the salad. Toss again.

Divide the salad between the plates and finish off by drizzling the rest of the hot green salsa over the top. I like to serve this with a small bowl of sour cream to cool it down and to dip the tortilla chips.

Swap in ... Add a little fried bacon for a more filling version.

This salad is straight out of a fantasy in my head because I adore hot Camembert so much and this recipe produces crunchy cheese slices that are golden on the outside and molten inside. The salad is really a vehicle for the little nuggets of crispy cheese that appear in the body of the leaves. The cherries are a seasonal cheat since they come from a jar, but the sourness is heaven with the Camembert.

For 4:
583 calories per portion
1½ of your five-a-day
For 6:
388 calories per portion
1 of your five-a-day

Crispy Camembert with Morello Cherry Vinaigrette *for Aunty Sarah*

Serves 4, or 6 as a starter

1 x 250g whole Camembert (not too ripe is best)

2 large free-range eggs, beaten lightly with a fork

125g white breadcrumbs (the cheaper and drier, the better)

3 tbsp vegetable oil

3 big handfuls spinach leaves, washed and dried

3 big handfuls mixed-leaf lettuce, washed and dried

1 red onion, finely chopped

30 walnut halves, roughly chopped and toasted in a dry frying pan

For the dressing

4 tbsp Morello cherry preserve

2 tbsp red wine vinegar

1 tbsp walnut oil

a pinch salt

Cut the Camembert wheel into 12 pieces. Dip the cheese slices in first the egg, then the breadcrumbs. Repeat once more so that each slice has been dunked in egg and breadcrumbs twice.

Heat up the oil in a large frying pan until hot but not smoking. Fry the breaded Camembert slices for a few minutes on each side, until golden and crispy. If you want to make this ahead, keep the fried cheese slices in the freezer and reheat in a very hot oven (220°C/425°F/gas mark 7) for 8 minutes, just before serving.

Meanwhile, make the cherry vinaigrette by heating up all the ingredients in a small saucepan and stirring to combine. Set aside to cool.

Once the cheese is ready, toss the leaves, red onion and walnuts in three quarters of the cooled dressing.

Serve with the cheese pieces dotted in the salad and drizzled with the remaining vinaigrette.

Swap in … Replace the walnuts with pecans and play around with the leaves. Replace the red onion with chives or finely chopped shallots. If you don't want to use spinach, use any dark green salad leaves that are tender.

It's 4 January – the first day back to work after the Christmas binge – and I'm staring at the empty fridge wondering what to make. The only significant item is the tail end of a block of Stilton. This is very much a leftovers salad, so feel free to use whatever leaves you have lying around in the fridge. I like the darker, slightly bitter leaves, like oak leaf, that cling to the dressing and deliver a sharp hit. This mountain of dark leaves soothes and softens the end of the hols.

312 calories per portion
1 of your five-a-day

Stilton and Apple Salad

Serves 2

2 large handfuls dark mixed leaves (such as oak leaf lettuce – avoid crunchy varieties), washed and spun dry

60g Stilton, crumbled roughly

40g shelled walnuts, toasted in a dry pan until golden

1 medium-sweet apple (Braeburn or Cox is ideal), cored and thinly sliced

a small handful chives, finely chopped

For the dressing

1 tsp sharp mustard (such as Colman's)

½ tsp runny honey

½ tsp olive oil

2 tsp cider vinegar

salt and pepper, to taste

First make the dressing by whisking together the mustard with the honey, then adding the olive oil. Finally, whisk in the vinegar and season to taste.

In the bottom of a big bowl, toss the leaves until lightly dressed. Next add the Stilton pieces, walnuts, apple slices and chives. Toss with the tips of your fingers until all the ingredients are roughly distributed. Divide between two plates and eat straight away.

Swap in ... This salad is also delicious with pear instead of apple. You could include a little chopped celery if you want.

As a rule, I'm not a fan of the whole *canard à l'orange* vibe and find that the oranges tend to overpower the duck. Tangerines, on the other hand, are more fragrant and sweeter. This salad is refreshing and rich in flavours. It's perfect on a cold January evening, with a glass of red wine and someone fun to talk to.

300 calories per portion
1 of your five-a-day

Duck and Tangerine Salad

Serves 4

1 very large or 2 smaller
 duck breasts

4 tangerines, peeled

90g seeded baguette bread
 (stale is best), roughly torn
 into bite-size pieces

1 tbsp olive oil

1 large clove garlic, minced

salt, to taste

2 generous handfuls
 watercress, washed and
 spun dry

2 handfuls lamb's lettuce,
 washed and spun dry

a small handful chives,
 finely chopped

For the rub

½ tsp pink peppercorns

½ tsp ground nutmeg

1 star anise

For the dressing

juice of 2 tangerines

2 tsp Dijon mustard

½ tsp runny honey

2 tbsp red wine vinegar

2 tbsp olive oil

Make the rub by pounding the spices together in a mortar and pestle, then transfer to a large plate. Press the duck breast into the spices and rub them in with your hands until the duck is well covered on both sides.

Put the duck fat side down in a cold pan and bring up to medium high. The fat will render out as the temperature rises. Fry until golden brown on both sides – roughly 15 minutes from start to finish for two small breasts; if the duck breast is on the large side fry for up to 20 minutes. Make a thin cut into the meat to see if it's done. I like mine very pink.

Whilst the duck is cooking, break the tangerines into segments. Slice off the flat edge of each segment. This removes the hardest edge of the fruit, so the slice will pop inside your mouth when you take a bite.

To make the dressing, boil the tangerine juice in a small saucepan for about 5 minutes, or until there is around 1 tbsp left. Add the mustard, honey, red wine vinegar and olive oil and whisk to combine. There is only a small amount of dressing, but a little goes a long way.

When the duck is done, wrap it in foil and let it relax until the rest of the salad ingredients are ready. Tip any remaining fat out of the pan. Add the roughly torn bread and 1 tbsp olive oil to the pan. Cook over a medium-high heat until the bread is toasted, then add the minced garlic and continue to cook for another minute. Remove from the pan.

Remove the duck from the foil and season with salt. Cut into slim slices. Toss the salad leaves in the warm dressing in a big bowl. Add the duck, the tangerine slices and the garlic croutons. Divide between four plates and sprinkle with a generous handful of chives. Serve warm.

Swap in ··· Pre-cooked and sliced smoked duck, warmed in a pan. Replace the croutons with toasted almonds for a gluten-free version.

This idea came from my wonderful editor, Becky. She's absolutely right: the book was missing a salad for when you're feeling rubbish and you need your food to bring you back from the brink. This is a recipe that's easy, comforting and nutritious. The hint of spice will put you back in touch with your taste buds, and the lemon, honey and tahini dressing will soothe and nurse you back to health.

683 calories per portion
2 of your five-a-day

Florence Nightingale Falafel Salad *for Mrs Wright*

Serves 1 poorly person and 1 saintly nurse – so 2 hearty helpings

1 small sweet potato, peeled and cut into small chunks

1 tbsp olive oil, mixed with 1 tsp rose harissa

6 falafels

2 large handfuls spinach leaves, washed and drained

a small handful flat-leaf parsley

For the dressing

3 tbsp tahini paste

1 small clove garlic, minced to a paste

1 tbsp freshly squeezed lemon juice

1 tsp runny honey

1 tsp olive oil

a pinch cayenne pepper

salt, to taste

Preheat the oven to 200°C/400°F/gas mark 6.

Make the dressing by combining all the ingredients and seasoning generously with salt.

Toss the sweet potato in the olive oil and harissa mixture, then cook on a baking sheet in the middle of the hot oven for 15 minutes, until golden. Add the falafels to the sweet potato and cook for a further 10 minutes.

Cool for a few minutes before adding the spinach and parsley. Drizzle generously with the tahini dressing and serve straight away.

Swap in ... You could dispense totally with the sweet potato and heat the falafel (double the quantities) in the microwave if you're at death's door and can't be bothered with the hassle of waiting for the oven.

Also, I think that the hint of chilli that you get from the harissa is essential, so if you can't find any or don't have any in the house at short notice, just use chilli flakes or chilli oil instead. Chilli is great for when you're bunged up, as it's a terrific decongestant.

Oooh! And I made this salad with feta crumbled over the top as well, which was WONDERFUL. As a rule, dairy isn't great for the system when you're congested but if you do ever want to try it with feta chunks, I highly recommend it.

My sister is mad about potato salad and this is her favourite version. The nigella seeds (also known as black onion seeds) really make the recipe. The chief problem with most potato salads I come across is that they tend to be claggy and caked in mayonnaise. The sour cream helps to freshen the recipe and let the flavour of the potato come through, and Désirée are naturally buttery.

217 calories per portion

Hot Potato Salad with Garlic and Nigella Seeds *for Mrs P*

Serves 4

600g Désirée potatoes, scrubbed

50g mayonnaise (I like Hellmann's)

1 heaped tbsp sour cream

1 small clove garlic, minced

½ tsp nigella seeds

salt and white pepper

a small handful chives, finely snipped

Boil the potatoes until tender. It helps if you pick potatoes that are roughly the same size, as they will all cook at the same speed.

Once cooked, cut into similar-sized chunks, then add the mayonnaise, sour cream, garlic and nigella seeds. The mayonnaise will go straight into the potatoes' flesh and disappear whilst the seeds will start infusing the salad. Season with salt and a little white pepper.

When the potatoes are warm but no longer boiling hot, scatter the snipped chives over the top. Serve still warm.

Swap in ... If you can't get hold of nigella seeds, use poppy seeds and bruised caraway seeds (done in a mortar and pestle) instead. You could replace the garlic and chives with spring onions.

780 calories per portion
2½ of your five-a-day

Serves 6

3 tbsp vegetable oil + 2 tsp
at the end

450g dried Puy lentils,
rinsed under the tap and
patted dry

As an alternative to the traditional recipe made with rice, I sometimes like to make kedgeree with lentils, a pulse that works wonderfully well with all the other Indian spices in this dish. This hearty recipe is tailor-made for office lunch boxes when you are craving a comforting, nutritious salad that will pluck you from the chilly winter and plonk you straight into the colourful, aromatic Indian warmth.

Lentil and Leek Kedgeree with Smoked Mackerel

6 leeks, finely sliced

8 cardamom, husks
removed, bashed
to a powder

2 cloves

2 cinnamon sticks

4 bay leaves

2 tsp ground allspice

2 tsp medium curry powder
(I like medium Madras)

salt and black pepper

a large handful flat-leaf
parsley, roughly chopped

600g smoked mackerel
fillets, skinned, boned
and broken into chunks

3 large free-range eggs,
boiled for 7 minutes

4 spring onions, chopped

1 lemon, cut into 6 wedges

a pinch cayenne pepper

8 tbsp sour cream, chives
snipped over (optional)

Heat the oil in a large pan and fry the rinsed lentils, leeks, cardamom, cloves, cinnamon sticks, bay leaves, allspice and curry powder over a low heat for 20 minutes.

Add 700ml water to the pan and cover the whole lot with a lid. Cook for a further 30 minutes, until the lentils are cooked and there is no water left in the pan. If you find that your lentils want another 10 minutes, add a small splash of water to the pan before letting them go further. Discard the bay leaves, cinnamon sticks and cloves. Adjust the seasoning and add the 2 tsp oil.

Fork the lentils and leeks to help cool them down before you add the parsley, flaked mackerel, eggs (halved) and spring onions to the rest of the salad.

Squeeze the lemon juice over and sprinkle with cayenne pepper before serving with the sour cream and chives on the side (if using).

Swap in ... Smoked haddock for mackerel, baked whilst the lentils are cooking. Swap the lentils for a mixture of basmati rice and lentils, or just rice. Add turmeric to the rice (if using).

Ally Fishman introduced me to the delights of orzo pasta, which is perfect for someone like me who doesn't like pasta salads too heavy. This is another perfect office lunch to take in a Tupperware and reheat. Simply add the mint at the last minute in that instance.

442 calories per portion
2½ of your five-a-day

Orzo Pasta with Roasted Squash, Pine Nuts and Mint

Serves 4

800g squash, washed, de-seeded and cut into medium chunks

2 tbsp olive oil

180g orzo pasta

40g pine nuts

freshly squeezed juice of 1 large lemon

plenty of salt and black pepper

a large bunch mint leaves

100g feta, crumbled

Preheat the oven to 220°C/425°F/gas mark 7.

Toss the squash in the olive oil and place on a baking tray at the top of the hot oven. Cook for 15 minutes, then switch the dial to 'grill' and colour the squash for a further 10 minutes.

Meanwhile, cook the pasta according to packet instructions. Drain and set aside. Toast the pine nuts in a dry frying pan until golden.

When the squash is cooked and golden, remove from the oven and add the pine nuts and orzo.

Squeeze the lemon juice over and season with salt and pepper. Just before serving, add the fresh mint and the feta.

Swap in ... Replace the squash with a mixture of courgette and pumpkin. You could also add 1 tsp ground allspice to the salad for a slightly Middle Eastern twist. If you can't find orzo, I recommend going for another small pasta shape instead.

This little physalis recipe is an example of something fun and flamboyant you can do with chocolate. I had been dreaming of ways of combining my love for chocolate with this sensational little fruit when the thought hit me that a chocolate-covered physalis would look exactly like a truffle. I have tried out many options for the 'truffle' flavours, but here are my two favourites.

White choc and hazelnut:
40 calories per truffle
Milk choc and pistachio:
38 calories per truffle

Physalis Chocolate Truffles

Makes around 12 truffles

White chocolate and hazelnut

50g white chocolate, broken into chunks

100g physalis

25g hazelnuts, chopped and roasted

Milk chocolate and pistachio

50g milk chocolate, broken into chunks

100g physalis

25g pistachios, chopped

Line a large plate with baking paper.

Set a heatproof bowl over boiling water and add the chocolate to it. Once completely melted, remove from the heat.

Open the papery shell around the fruit by holding it with your fingers and opening it just like a packet of crisps. Carefully fold back the paper outer skin to reveal the fruit inside. Give each orange ball a quick wipe with kitchen paper, as the skin tends to be a little waxy and can prevent the chocolate from sticking.

Using the outer paper of the fruit as a holding device, dip the fruit in the chocolate followed by the nuts if using. Set down on the baking paper.

Once all the 'truffles' have been coated, refrigerate for 2 hours to set before serving.

These physalis 'truffles' make a sensational *petit four* to go with coffee at the end of dinner or lunch.

Swap in ... White chocolate and crushed freeze-dried strawberries are a lovely combination. Also, try using dark chocolate and dip the tip of the truffle in cocoa powder or very finely chopped stem ginger.

427 calories per portion
2 of your five-a-day

Serves 6

1kg boneless pork
shoulder joint with rind on

1 tsp salt

ground white pepper

50g light muscovado sugar

I am crazy for alliteration and these 3 Ps were too much to resist, especially when I discovered how wonderfully well they suit each other. Pulled pork is something I discovered in the US and tends to be associated with the mighty barbecue sphere of food, although it's also quite common to find recipes for pulled pork that are done on the stove top or in the oven, like this one.

Pulled Pork and Pomegranate

1 tbsp fennel seeds,
bruised in a mortar
and pestle

1 tbsp Chinese five-spice

250ml water

5 cloves garlic, bashed

2 large heads pak choi,
cut into very fine strips
lengthways

seeds from 2 medium
pomegranates

6 spring onions, sliced
thinly on the diagonal

8 pink radish, cut into
matchsticks

1 cucumber, peeled,
de-seeded and cut into
long matchsticks

2 medium-sized green
chillies, most of the seeds
removed, very finely diced

For the dressing

2 tbsp Thai fish sauce

80ml rice or malt vinegar

30g light muscovado sugar

2 tbsp dark soy sauce

4 tbsp vegetable oil

Preheat the oven to 150°C/300°F/gas mark 2.

Put the pork in an ovenproof saucepan that has a lid and add the salt, a good pinch of white pepper, sugar, fennel seeds and Chinese five-spice. Rub the spices over the meat and add the water and garlic at the bottom of the pan. Cook in the bottom of the oven for 4 hours, then remove the lid and cook for the remaining hour.

When the meat has had its full time, remove from the oven and turn on the grill. Grill the meat (rind side up) in the middle of the oven until blistered and golden brown – between 5 and 10 minutes. Then remove the rind with a knife and scrape off any extra fat from the meat. Chop the 'crackling' into strips and add to the meat.

Using two forks, pull the pork into shreds and moisten with 4 tbsp of the juices from the pan, which will have reduced and intensified.

Next, add the pak choi to the warm pork and let it sit for a few minutes to wilt whilst you mix together the remaining salad ingredients.

Add the salad to the pan with the pork and pak choi. Briefly toss before piling on to your serving platter.

To make the dressing, simply mix all the ingredients in a clean jam jar and give a good shake. Serve with the dressing drizzled over the top.

Swap in … This is fun piled into little pancakes (like the ones used in Peking Duck) and served with plum sauce. You can also replace some or all of the pak choi with fennel, for a change.

I'm an all-or-nothing person . . . so when I fell in love I put on 10 lb in eight weeks. It was a while before I realized the size of the problem, but when I did I had to digest my disbelief and get cracking on finding fun ways of eating *à deux* whilst losing the extra. This is the salad for when you just want something lively, green and virtuous to go with a juicy steak.

106 calories per portion
1½ of your five-a-day

Salad that Goes with Steak (Lean and Mean)

Serves 1

a large handful dark, mixed leaves

40g sunblush tomatoes (also called semi-dried), drained of oil

a small handful chives, finely chopped

a small handful tarragon, finely chopped

For the dressing

1 tsp olive oil

½ tsp balsamic vinegar

½ tsp freshly squeezed lemon juice

plenty of salt and pepper

Combine the dressing ingredients in a clean jam jar and give a good shake. Dress the leaves on your plate and scatter the tomatoes and herbs on top. Serve on the side of a beautiful, seared steak.

Swap in ... Add a little finely sliced onion or shallot, a few sprigs of parsley and ½ tsp of Dijon mustard to the dressing for a slightly French twist. It's also wonderful with a little garlic in the dressing, and is just as cracking with grilled or barbecued chicken.

This is a lovely combination of flavours and colours to warm up the winter months. I sometimes also like this salad with a little hit of chilli flakes, which I add to the squash whilst it's cooking. This recipe is a firm staple for me and I'm just as comfortable making a small amount for myself for a Tuesday telly night on my own as I am serving it at a dinner party.

206 calories per portion
2 of your five-a-day

Squash Salad with Pomegranate and Prosciutto

Serves 4

6 thin slices prosciutto, roughly torn with the fat removed

2 tsp olive oil

400g squash, peeled, de-seeded and cut into cubes

4 large handfuls rocket, rinsed and dried

seeds from 1 large pomegranate

20g Pecorino, shaved very finely

For the garlic cream dressing

1 clove garlic, minced

1 anchovy fillet, very finely chopped

2 tbsp half-fat crème fraîche

1 tsp mayonnaise (I like Hellmann's)

1 tsp Dijon mustard

1 tsp sherry vinegar

Place the prosciutto slices in a large, dry frying pan over a high heat and fry them until crispy on both sides – around 5 minutes. Set aside. They will get even more crispy as they cool down.

Next, heat the olive oil in the large frying pan and fry the squash chunks over a high heat. Once coloured, turn down the heat and put a lid over the pan. Cook for 5 minutes further with the lid on, or until the squash is tender but not disintegrating. Take the lid off and let the squash cool down a little before serving.

Meanwhile, make up the dressing by combining all the ingredients in a clean jam jar and giving a good shake.

When the squash is ready, add the rocket, prosciutto and pomegranate to the cooled pan and give a good stir to combine the leaves with the warm squash.

Divide between four plates and drizzle with the garlic cream dressing, which is meant to be quite thick. Scatter the Pecorino over before serving with some fresh ciabatta (olive is nice with this if you can find it).

Swap in ···· If you want to fly *sans* the prosciutto, I recommend using a little more Pecorino and a handful of seeds, like sunflower, that you toast in a frying pan with a little bit of soy sauce. The meat in this recipe has a role in delivering crunch and salt.

593 calories per portion
½ of your five-a-day

Serves 4

4 wood pigeon breasts,
   skin on

1 tbsp clear honey

salt and pepper

The winter is made for salads like this one. This recipe is great if two of you want to make lunch together or if you're in the mood for listening to the radio whilst pottering about in the kitchen. 'Smoking' meat is *really* fun and super-easy. It does tend to infuse the whole house, so beware if you're doing this right before your mates rock up for lunch!

Thyme-smoked Wood Pigeon and Pancetta

200g pancetta cubes

1 tbsp olive oil

4 large handfuls young red
   leaves (such as oak leaf
   lettuce), washed and dried

a small handful parsley,
   leaves only

For the smoke

2 tbsp Earl Grey tea leaves,
   or the contents of
   2 teabags

1 tbsp caster sugar

a small bunch thyme

3 tbsp rice (any kind)

For the garlic croutons

1 ciabatta roll, ripped into
   small chunks

15g butter

2 cloves garlic, finely sliced

For the dressing

3 tbsp Blueberry Balsamic
   Glaze (page 187)

1 tbsp walnut oil

Paint the underside (with no skin) of the pigeons with honey and crush over a little salt and pepper. To smoke them, place a double layer of tinfoil in the bottom of a wide saucepan and put the tea leaves, sugar, thyme and rice on the foil. Add a steamer to the bottom of the pan, just above the foil layer. Next, put the seasoned breasts in the steamer and place the lid over. Turn the heat under the pan to medium hot and smoke the meat for 10–12 minutes.

Whilst the pigeons are smoking, heat up a dry frying pan. Add the pancetta and fry over a high heat until crispy. Set aside. In the same pan (don't remove any of the fat from the pancetta), add the ciabatta chunks and fry over a medium heat until golden and crispy. Remove from the pan with a slotted spoon.

Next, add the butter and heat it until it foams before adding the slices of garlic. They will take around 1 minute to cook and turn golden, at which point you can take them out and add them to the pile of croutons.

Once the pigeon breasts have had their time, add them to the pan (skin side down) with 1 tbsp olive oil and fry for 2 minutes to crisp up the skin. Remove from the pan and cover in foil until the salad is ready.

Assemble the dressing ingredients in a large bowl and add the salad and parsley leaves. Toss, then divide between four plates. Slice the pigeon thinly and add to the salad, along with the pancetta and croutons.

Swap in … Pheasant or partridge for the pigeon. Swap in Balsamic Glaze (page 186) with a handful of flesh blueberries.

Ever since reading about the irrepressible Eloise who lived at the Plaza, I've had a nostalgic attraction to institutional old hotels, like the Waldorf Astoria. Because I don't enjoy salads that are *covered* in mayonnaise, I have doctored the texture, taste and amounts of dressing here. With the exception of a little winter twist of my own, the flavours are straight from the original recipe, attributed to Oscar Tschirky in 1896.

263 calories per portion
3 of your five-a-day

Waldorf Salad

Serves 4 as a starter

2 small red apples (such as Pink Lady or Gala), cored and diced into 1cm cubes

freshly squeezed juice of ½ lemon

60g pecan nuts, roughly chopped

1 head romaine lettuce, leaves washed and shredded

2 celery sticks, diced

100g seedless green grapes, rinsed under the tap and cut in half

For the dressing

3 tbsp yoghurt

3 tbsp mayonnaise (I like Hellmann's)

¼ tsp ground mixed spice

finely grated zest of ½ lemon

salt and pepper

Tip the diced apples into a large bowl and toss them in the lemon juice until all the pieces are coated. Set aside.

Toast the pecans in a dry frying pan over a medium heat until golden – roughly 6–8 minutes. Set aside to cool whilst you prepare the salad dressing.

Whisk together the ingredients for the dressing in a bowl, taste and season.

Next, add the dressing to the apples in the bowl and stir to combine. Add the shredded romaine lettuce and the celery, then toss again. Finally, sprinkle the grapes and toasted pecans over just before serving.

Swap in ... You can replace the pecans with walnuts and the grapes with raisins if preferred. The addition of the mixed spice is my own, but this salad is also lovely without it if eating at any other time of the year.

It's that time of year again when all I want to do at the end of the day is potter in my kitchen, sipping on a glass of red wine. This light salad is full of flavour and satisfies any cravings I get for rich, red meat. I like to use a mixture of warm chicory and peppy green leaves for this salad. The secret of the recipe lies in the balance of the bitter leaves, the rich meat and the sweet sharpness of the figs and Balsamic Glaze.

482 calories per portion
2½ of your five-a-day

Warm Salad of Chicken Livers and Chicory

Serves 2

220g chicken livers, trimmed of any sinew

200ml semi-skimmed milk

30g walnut halves, toasted in a dry frying pan

2 tsp walnut oil

2 small heads red chicory leaves, cut in half lengthways

1 small clove garlic, finely sliced

2 figs, cut into quarters

50g plain flour

salt and pepper

2 tbsp vegetable oil

1 handful oak leaf lettuce, leaves washed and dried

1 tbsp Balsamic Glaze (shop-bought, or see page 186)

a small handful chives, finely chopped

Soak the chicken livers in the milk for 15 minutes to soften the liver flavour.

Heat a large frying pan with 2 tsp of walnut oil. Once hot, add the chicory leaves, along with the garlic. Cook over a high heat for a minute to soften. Remove from the pan and set aside.

Whilst the pan is still hot, fry the figs for 1 minute, just to warm through and caramelize. Set aside.

Toss the wet livers in plain flour with a crunch of salt and pepper. Tap them gently to remove any excess flour. Heat the vegetable oil and add the floured livers. Cook over a medium heat until golden on both sides. I like mine pink in the middle, but it's up to you. If you want them underdone, it's best to cook over a higher heat for a shorter time.

Next, assemble the salad by tossing together the fresh oak leaf leaves, the warmed chicory leaves, toasted walnuts and chicken livers.

Finally, drizzle over the Balsamic Glaze and position the delicate figs so as to avoid them disintegrating completely. Scatter the chives and serve with a good crunch of salt and pepper.

Swap in ... Replace Balsamic Glaze with 1 tbsp balsamic vinegar, thickened with 1 tsp honey. This salad would also work with just oak leaf leaves, but add croutons to replace the crunch of chicory.

There are few colourful or flamboyant winter fruits, but luckily both oranges and pomegranates make up for it. This simple fruit salad is lovely as a light dessert. I also have it at breakfast when I want a hit of hot colours first thing. Because it lasts for days in the fridge, it's an easy one to make up and dip into when you feel like it. I recommend serving this with shop-bought ginger and chocolate biscuits at dinner parties.

140 calories per portion
2 of your five-a-day

Winter Fruit Salad of Orange and Pomegranate

Serves 4

6 juicy oranges (such as Jaffa or Navel)

seeds from 1 large pomegranate

For the ginger and cinnamon syrup

300ml water

50g caster sugar

freshly squeezed juice of ½ lemon

70g raw ginger, peeled and roughly chopped

1 cinnamon stick

To make the syrup, heat all the ingredients together in a small saucepan over a medium heat. Once the sugar has completely dissolved, boil hard for 6 minutes or until the liquid has reduced by half. Set aside to cool.

Whilst the syrup is reducing, cut the peel from the oranges, working from north to south (if you catch my drift). It's much easier to use a serrated knife for this job, as it will help you to waste as little orange as possible.

Slice the 'bald' oranges into thin strips across the waist and arrange in a serving bowl. Scatter the pomegranate seeds over. Finally, pour the cooled syrup over before serving.

Swap in ... Replace the pomegranate with dried cranberries, soaked in the warm, finished syrup for 10 minutes before serving. Scatter toasted pistachios over for a change of colour.

430 calories per portion
1½ of your five-a-day

Serves 2

200g waxy new potatoes,
  cut into 1cm dice

2 tsp olive oil

I like this robust salad in winter because, with its vibrant Sicilian undertones, it carries with it memories of sunshine. This recipe is perfect for dreaming of lemons when the pavements are covered in ice crystals and the wind cuts through your clothes. The good news is that it all takes place in one frying pan, so there's very little fuss or washing-up to do!

Spinach, Steak and Sautéed Potatoes

160g bavette/flank steak

5g butter

2 large handfuls baby
  spinach, rinsed and dried

For the Sicilian dressing

½ tsp Dijon mustard

1 tsp freshly squeezed
  lemon juice

1 tsp olive oil

30g pine nuts, toasted in
  a dry pan

1 clove garlic, finely minced

1 chilli, cut into very small
  dice

finely grated zest of ½
  unwaxed lemon

3 tsp capers, drained of
  brine

1 anchovy, finely sliced

120g cherry tomatoes on
  the vine, cut in half

a bunch basil, roughly
  chopped

plenty of salt and pepper

First fry the potato cubes in a hot, non-stick dry frying pan for 5 minutes. After the potato has been in the pan for 5 minutes, add 2 tsp olive oil and toss the hot potato to coat. Keep cooking over a high heat until well coloured all over and cooked through. This will take around 10 minutes. Once cooked, remove from the pan and set aside whilst you cook the steak.

Add the steak to the empty pan until well browned on one side (roughly 3 minutes). Next, add the butter to the pan and flip the steak over. Cook for another 3–5 minutes for a steak that's pink in the middle. Once cooked, wrap the steak in foil and rest for 5 minutes.

To make the Sicilian dressing, combine the mustard, lemon juice, olive oil, toasted pine nuts, minced garlic, chilli, lemon zest, capers, chopped anchovy, sliced tomatoes and basil in a big bowl. Season with salt and pepper.

Lightly toss the spinach and potatoes in half the dressing and then transfer to your serving dish. Next, slice the steak and lay it on top of the spinach. Finally, spoon over the remaining Sicilian dressing and serve warm.

Swap in ... You could use half a preserved lemon in this dressing instead of the zest. Also, replace the beef with lamb steak and the basil with parsley.

This recipe is a sloppy, soft salad that is comforting, elegant, easy and perfect for a winter lunchbox. I sometimes have it with a little grilled chicken on the side, but most of the time I love it on its own. You can also add diced chargrilled red peppers, a little chilli, some roasted butternut squash or a little fried tofu if the fancy takes you.

342 calories per portion
2 of your five-a-day

Winter Store-cupboard Salad
of mushroom, pearl barley and parsley

Serves 4

120g pearl barley

500ml chicken or vegetable stock

4 tbsp olive oil

1 white onion, cut into small dice

500g chestnut mushrooms, cleaned and cut into quarters

125ml white wine

2 bay leaves

2 tbsp capers

a large bunch curly parsley, finely chopped

plenty of salt and white pepper

Cook the pearl barley by covering it with water and bringing it to the boil, then draining it, covering it with the stock and bringing it to the boil a second time. Simmer for 30–40 minutes, until the grains are soft.

Heat 2 tbsp of the olive oil in a large frying pan and add the onion. Reduce the heat and fry for 10 minutes uncovered, or until the onion is translucent. Remove with a slotted spoon and set aside.

Next, heat another 1 tbsp of the olive oil in the empty frying pan until it starts to shimmer. At this point, add the mushrooms and cook over a high heat until they are browned. It's important not to crowd the mushrooms in the pan as they could sweat instead of searing. You may want to do this process in two stages.

Once the mushrooms are golden and softened, add the white wine, bay leaves, cooked barley and onion. Simmer gently for 10 minutes with the lid on. Remove the bay leaves.

Finally, remove from the heat and allow to cool for 10 minutes. Combine the warm mixture with the remaining 1 tbsp of olive oil, the capers and chopped parsley. Season generously with salt and white pepper before serving. Keeps well for up to 3 days in the fridge.

Swap in ... You can add in soft-boiled eggs (halved) or fried pancetta cubes to this for a slightly more filling lunch.

Glazes, Dressings, Pestos and Vinegars

Glazes

Balsamic Glaze

Makes 200ml
36 calories per tbsp

Preheat the oven to 200°C/400°F/gas mark 6.
Place a clean kilner jar or ovenproof bottle with its
lid beside it in the middle of the oven for
10 minutes to sterilize. Set aside to cool.

Pour **500ml balsamic vinegar** into a medium
saucepan and turn the heat to high. Once it comes
to the boil, reduce the heat and simmer gently for
30 minutes. The bubbles will get bigger towards
the end of the cooking time.

You can expect the liquid to have reduced by half.
It is ready when the glaze will coat the back of a
teaspoon dipped into it. Decant into the sterilized
jar and allow to cool.

Blueberry Balsamic Glaze

Makes 250ml
22 calories per tbsp

Preheat the oven to 200°C/400°F/gas mark 6. Place a clean 600ml jar with its lid beside it in the hot oven for 10 minutes to sterilize. Set aside to cool.

Heat **200g blueberries** and **250ml balsamic vinegar** in a saucepan to boiling point. Turn down the heat and simmer gently for 5 minutes more. The liquid should look thickened but should not coat the back of a spoon.

Remove from the heat and strain into the sterilized jar, little by little, pushing the fruit through the sieve with the back of a spoon. Allow to stand for 10 minutes. If you don't like bits, strain again; if you don't mind a slightly grainy look, don't bother as it won't affect the taste.

Sweet Chilli and Tomato Glaze

Makes 400ml
20 calories per tbsp

Preheat the oven to 200°C/400°F/gas mark 6. Place a clean jar with its lid beside it in the oven for 10 minutes to sterilize. Allow to cool.

Gently warm **300ml white wine vinegar** in a saucepan with ½ **tsp salt** and **300g caster sugar**, stirring to dissolve.

Scoop out the centres of **10 cherry tomatoes** (cut in half across the waist) and discard. Roughly chop. Add the tomatoes and **5 red chillies**, halved and finely chopped (I retain the seeds of 2 for hotness), to the vinegar pan and turn up the heat. Simmer uncovered for 15 minutes. You will have a glossy, thickened glaze. Carefully pour into the jar. The glaze will thicken as it cools. Store in a cool place.

Dressings

Balsamic Vinaigrette

Makes 120ml
32 calories per tbsp

Put **2 tbsp extra-virgin olive oil, 1 tbsp balsamic vinegar, 1 tbsp freshly squeezed lemon juice** and **plenty of salt and pepper** in a clean jar and give it a good shake until everything is combined.

Light Caesar Dressing

Makes 400ml
65 calories per tbsp

Put **120g mayonnaise** (I like Hellmann's), **8 drained and finely chopped anchovies, 4 minced cloves garlic** and **120ml freshly squeezed lemon juice** in a clean jar and shake until loose and combined. Add **60g plain full-fat yoghurt, 4 tsp Dijon mustard, 4 tbsp olive oil, 2 tsp Worcestershire sauce** and **a pinch celery salt** and shake again. Keeps 3–5 days in a jar in the fridge.

Vietnamese Sweet and Sour Dressing

Makes 125ml
28 calories per tbsp

Put **4 tbsp fish sauce, 3 tbsp freshly squeezed
lime juice, 3 tsp rice vinegar, 3 tbsp caster sugar**
and **½ small red chilli** (de-seeded and very finely
diced) in a clean jar and stir to combine. Optional
additional ingredients include: 100ml lychee syrup
(from tinned lychees) or 100ml water, 1 bruised and
finely chopped lemongrass stem, 1 finely chopped
spring onion, 1cm peeled and finely grated root
ginger and 1 tbsp very finely diced carrot.

Swiss Vinaigrette

Makes 100ml
48 calories per tbsp

Shake **4 tsp Dijon mustard, 2 tbsp olive oil,
2 tbsp red wine vinegar, 1 tsp runny honey** and
a pinch salt in a clean jam jar until combined.

Pestos

Lime and Coriander Pesto

Makes 4 generous servings
368 calories per portion

Blitz **4 handfuls fresh coriander** and **1 peeled clove garlic** in a food processor with **100ml olive oil**. Add **50g shelled pistachios** and blitz briefly to chop the nuts roughly. I like a bit of chop to my pesto, so I add **50g of finely grated fresh Manchego** by hand.

Add **35ml freshly squeezed lime juice** (roughly the juice of 1 large lime), season well with **plenty of salt and pepper** and stir. Tip into a clean jar and keep for up to a week in the fridge.

Red Pepper Pesto

Makes 4 servings
120 calories per portion

Whizz **2 chargrilled red peppers, 2 cloves garlic, 30g sunblush tomatoes, 2 tsp chilli flakes** and **30g pine nuts** in a food processor for 10 seconds. Scrape down the sides and whizz for 10 seconds more – longer if you like it smooth. Stir in **40g finely grated fresh Pecorino**, loosen with **2 tbsp freshly squeezed lemon juice** and season with **a pinch salt**. Keeps in the fridge for up to 3 days. If it stiffens, loosen with a little extra olive oil and lemon juice.

Hazelnut Pesto

Makes 4 servings
316 calories per portion

Preheat the oven to 200°C/400°F/gas mark 6. Roast
30g whole blanched hazelnuts on a baking sheet
for 5 minutes in the middle of the hot oven, until
golden and fragrant. Set aside to cool.

Blitz **60g basil** in a food processor with **100ml olive
oil**. Add the hazelnuts and blitz briefly to chop the nuts
roughly. Stir in **40g finely grated fresh Parmesan**.

Add **35ml freshly squeezed lemon juice** (roughly
the juice of 1 lemon), season well with **plenty of salt
and pepper** and stir. Keep in a jar in the fridge for up
to a week. Before using, remove from the fridge for
an hour and stir well to combine.

Vinegars

Honey and Tarragon Vinegar

Makes 500ml
6.5 calories per tbsp

Preheat the oven to 200°C/400°F/gas mark 6. Place a 500ml heatproof glass container with its lid next to it in the middle of the hot oven to sterilize. Remove after 10 minutes and cool.

Bring **500ml white wine vinegar** to the boil in a stainless-steel saucepan. Remove from the heat and pour into the sterilized container, add **a small handful tarragon leaves** and **2 tbsp strong, set honey** (I use heather honey), then screw on the lid tightly. Store in a dark, cool place for 2 weeks before using. Stir before using, to make sure that the flavours are evenly distributed.

Raspberry Vinegar

Makes 600ml
4 calories per tbsp

Preheat the oven to 200°C/400°F/gas mark 6. Place a large heatproof jar with its lid next to it in the middle of the oven to sterilize for 10 minutes. Allow to cool.

Bring **500ml red wine vinegar** to the boil in a stainless-steel saucepan, then add **440g raspberries** and set aside to cool and infuse for an hour or so. Strain the mixture through a sieve. If you want to remove all impurities, strain again through muslin.

Decant into the sterilized jar and keep in the fridge.

Thyme and Tangerine Vinegar

Makes 500ml

3 calories per tbsp

Preheat the oven to 200°C/400°F/gas mark 6. Place a large heatproof container with its lid next to it in the middle of the hot oven to sterilize. Remove after 10 minutes and allow to cool.

Bring **500ml cider vinegar** to the boil in a stainless-steel saucepan. Remove from the heat and pour into the sterilized container. Add **a handful thyme** and **zest of 2 tangerines**, then screw on the lid tightly. Store in a dark, cool place for 2 weeks before using.

Cucumber and Pink Peppercorn Vinegar

Makes 600ml

3 calories per tbsp

Preheat the oven to 200°C/400°F/gas mark 6. Place a large heatproof container with its lid next to it in the middle of the hot oven to sterilize. Remove after 10 minutes and allow to cool.

Bring **500ml white wine vinegar** to the boil in a stainless-steel saucepan. Remove from the heat and pour into the sterilized jar. Add ½ **small cucumber**, washed and finely sliced, and **2 tsp pink peppercorns**, then seal tightly. Leave for a week before using.

Index

If this book is such a delight to look at, it's because of the terrific talent of Tap Tap Hawkins, Loopy Laura, Joss Herd and Lucy Gowans. Each in your own ways, you knew what I meant even when I didn't know it myself. Thank you for making every shoot day a party and for pouring yourselves into these pages.

Becky Jones (now Mrs Wright!) is the secret sauce behind the books since *Red Velvet & Chocolate Heartache*. Thank you for going above and beyond, Becky, for believing and for understanding from the beginning.

Thank you to Felicity Blunt and Rebecca Ritchie at Curtis Brown for your dynamism, energy and great gut instincts. I feel lucky to have you both on the home team.

I am indebted to Transworld for enabling me to do a job I love and for continuing to have faith in my ideas. Doug, I blame you. Other stars over at TW Towers include Polly, Elizabeth, Bella and brilliant Brenda. Thanks for all your hard work.

I want to thank Sophio, Sarah and Johnny Van Haeften for welcoming me home after Paris as well as for eating mountains of salad with a smile and helping me tweak my recipes for the better!

Danny Maguire, you have been a rock star assistant … You are everywhere in this book. After you left on some of our testing days, I felt so grateful that I would have given you my house or my lungs (my liver's not worth much!). I couldn't have done it without you.

I get sunbeams of support from the following people: Georgie Porgie Parr, Max, Papa, Mummy, and beautiful baby Otto. Thank you for guiding me and for looking after me.

Lastly: Minnesota. Thank God for Taco Night.